THE FIRE IS FOR YOU

Travis Hearn

FREE GIFTS

Scan here to access your free gifts!

Hear Pastor Travis' story in his own words as he reads Chapter 1 of "The Fire Is for You," take a deeper dive into themes and topics explored in this book with a special hand-picked sermon series, listen in as Pastor Travis answers key questions about the book and shares personal reflections on his experience, and download your exclusive, printable journal!

DEDICATION

This book is dedicated to anyone who needs a miracle in their life. I am a walking and breathing testimony that God is a miracle worker, and that He still does modern-day miracles to this day. He is able. And He can do the impossible. So hang on, don't lose faith, and keep trusting and believing God that your miracle is on the way. He is the miracle.

ACKNOWLEDGMENTS

"Miracles, signs, and wonders…these signs will follow those who believe. Pastor Travis Hearn is a living, breathing testimony of this reality. The words from the pages of this book inspired my faith, encouraged my soul, and challenged me to believe God for the impossible!"

Tauren Wells
10X Grammy Nominated Artist and Pastor

"From his life-changing diagnosis to his miraculous healing, Pastor Travis' story puts the wonder-working power of Almighty God on full display. What happened here really is the true definition of a miracle. I recommend this book for anyone needing God to do something big in their lives!"

Stephen Chandler
Author and Senior Pastor, Union Church

"When I heard of Pastor Travis' stroke, I immediately felt called to reach out and help as I am not only a Doctor of Physical Therapy, but I also specialize in neurologic conditions. And I'm happy I did because I got to witness a miracle. Travis' stroke happened in a notoriously life-threatening area, the brain stem, which is responsible for all functions of human life. I thought the miracle would be that he lived. Strokes of this magnitude often take months to years to improve and don't often heal. Yet, in a matter of weeks, Travis was running, jumping, and planning his first sermon back. I have never seen healing of that magnitude and I know it was God's healing because it was humanly impossible. The miracle wasn't just that he lived, it was so much more. What Travis did next with his life shows that the healing powers of God extend far beyond human capacity."

Dr. Ashley Will, PT, DPT, NCS

"Pastor Travis has been in the trenches and come out on the other side with a story to tell. The Fire Is for You is not only a personal account of all that he went through, it's a powerful tool filled with biblical truths to stand on no matter what type of battle you face! If you are hurting or struggling today, this book is a must read!"

Chad Veach
Author and Lead Pastor, Zoe Church

"When you see something that completely defies what medicine says is possible, the only place to look is to God. Travis' amazing story shows us the truth: that God really does work miracles, against all odds. As both a physician and friend, I am in awe of Travis' faith, results, and testimony, and hope this story inspires all who read it. All glory and praise to God!"

Dr. Sabrina Solt, ND

"Pastor Travis is my pastor, my friend, and at the time of his stroke, he was my NBA chaplain as well. As we received news of his stroke, we were confronted with the grim possibilities and severity of the situation. I vividly remember our team getting on FaceTime with him as we and many others prayed for his health. I had a front row seat to a portion of his recovery, and I watched as he began to heal and improve. This experience had a profound impact on my faith, and I believe that as you read this book, it will deeply impact yours as well."

Cameron Johnson
NBA Player

"The Fire Is for You will not only give you a whole new perspective on the trials of life, it will inspire anyone who's going through a battle to keep going, keep fighting, and keep trusting God that their victory is on the way! This is such a powerful read!"

Tracy Cortez
UFC Fighter

"Travis Hearn is a man of incredible character, faith, and leadership. Over the years, I've watched him lead with authenticity and a heart for people that is truly rare. Whether he's pastoring, mentoring, or just being a friend, Travis brings a spirit of humility and strength to everything he does. His faith isn't just something he preaches; it's how he lives, even in the face of life's greatest challenges. Travis is a leader who makes others better, and his life is a powerful testimony of God's grace and resilience. I'm grateful to call him a brother and witness how he continues to impact so many lives."

Pastor Mike Todd
Transformation Church, New York Times Best Selling Author

======

"It takes a special anointing to walk through fire and not smell like smoke. Travis lived it, and shares his tragedy to triumph story in this book. These pages not only contain a spiritual GPS for healing, they provide a template to find joy in the midst of life's biggest challenges. We've been fortunate to have floor seats to this miracle, and the miracles that continue to come when you know The Fire Is for You."

Montell & Kristin Jordan

Grammy Award Winning Recording Artist, Authors, and Marriage Pastors

======

"I've been through some fires in my life, and I continue to learn time and time again that there's always a reason for my fires, and that God always has a purpose for my pain. I've learned that the fires of life are where I'm refined and purified. The pressures of life are where I'm developed and made strong. The fire is always FOR me and not against me. And that God's not done with me yet. If you're going through a fire in your own life today, I know that this book will help you to see the same. Pastor Travis' story will not only reframe your perspective, it will forever change the way you look at life's fires!"

Odell Beckham Jr.

NFL Player

======

Acknowledgments

"Pastor Trav is not just a friend. His faithfulness, prayer, and surrender to our Savior Jesus Christ make him an inspiration. I personally watched PT, and his family, walk step-by-step through a tough medical situation. They never wavered. They trusted through the tough stuff. They pointed people to Jesus, even when it wasn't going well for them. I am grateful to call him a friend and I know that this book will be a blessing to you and your family... LET'S GO!"

Monty Williams
NBA Player, NBA Coach

"Overcoming one of the most devastating unexpected setbacks, Travis Hearn uses his personal testimony and experiences to masterfully coach all those who need a second wind and a push to their next! I highly recommend this book to anyone who refuses to let any type of setback have the last say in their life!"

Danny Gokey
Multi-Grammy Nominated Artist and Songwriter

"The Fire Is for You by Travis Hearn is a powerful testimony of the faithfulness of God in the darkest night. His personal journey will deeply encourage you and lift your eyes to where your hope comes from. Travis reminds us that the love of God and the gift of His ever present Spirit brings supernatural strength to our hearts no matter how impossible or devastating our circumstance. You will be reminded that you never walk alone!"

Pastor Rich Wilkerson Jr.
Senior Pastor, VOUS Church

The Fire Is for You

TABLE OF CONTENTS

INTRODUCTION

"Now, don't be crying when I leave—I will be right back." Those were the words Travis said to me as he was being wheeled away to the ambulance on Monday, November 14, 2022. And they turned out to be the last words he would say to me before my world came crashing down.

The day started like any normal, uneventful Monday. We typically have Mondays off together, so we had spent the morning running errands, grabbing coffees, and getting cold plunges.

As the day went on, I noticed that Travis was a little quiet, but that wasn't unusual; I often teased him about being quiet on Mondays after using up all of his words on Sundays. I assumed that he was just tired after the long weekend, and I didn't think much of it after that.

But when I received a text from him later that afternoon and saw that the words were slightly jumbled, I immediately knew that something wasn't right. So, I headed to the store where he was shopping with our youngest daughter, and asked him to come home with me right away.

I know it may have seemed a little extreme in the moment considering his speech was fine and he seemed fairly normal (besides continuously dropping his phone), but I just knew in my spirit that he was having a stroke.

After we arrived at home, I convinced Travis to let me call emergency services, and not long after that, he was on his way to the hospital to get checked out.

Introduction

As I waited for our son to make the short drive home to be with his younger sister while I went to the hospital, I prayed that Travis was right and that he would be home soon with a clean bill of health. Unfortunately, that is not how things turned out.

I was just getting the kids settled when I received a phone call that I will never forget. A doctor from the hospital was calling to inform me that Travis had a major brain bleed and would need to be taken to a trauma one center by helicopter.

I was in shock as I headed to the hospital just minutes later, and I had no idea what to expect when I arrived. But I was definitely not prepared for what was waiting for me in that hospital room.

The last time I had seen Travis, he was telling me not to worry and that everything would be fine. But now, just 30 minutes later, he had lost all ability to speak and things were not looking good.

As we waited for the helicopter to arrive, I tried to keep Travis calm. I could see that things were moving quickly downhill, not only with his speech, but with his mental capacity, as well.

Finally, after what seemed like an eternity, they were ready to transport him to the trauma center. So, we walked him out to the helicopter, I kissed him goodbye, and then it was back to the car to race over and meet him there.

I will never forget that first night in the ICU. It was terrifying! We had no idea what was going on, and the hospital staff could not yet answer any of our questions or tell us what might be in store for our future.

I was thankful for one hospital employee that entered the room in the middle of the night when I was attempting to sleep in a chair while holding Trav's hand. He scooted the bed and the chair closer together and lowered the bed rail so that I could reach Travis better.

He told me not to be surprised if things got worse before getting better, because stroke healing was not linear. I never saw or spoke to that young employee again, but when Trav got worse, I held on to his words in my heart.

The next few days were a blur of difficult and emotional moments, and I did not want to leave Travis' side. He was still totally unable to communicate with anyone around him, but because I had been married to him for a quarter of a century, I was able to distinguish what he wanted and needed when others could not. "In sickness and in health" became very real for us in those moments.

When the neurologist informed me that the effects of this type of stroke are typically irreversible, I had to fight the fear that began rising up inside of me. I had to remember that our mighty God is not "typical" and does not work in statistics. He works in the miraculous.

So, in those difficult moments, I held on to the Word of God and stood on Acts 3:16 (NIV), "By faith in the name of Jesus, this man whom you see and know was made strong. It is Jesus' name and the faith that comes through him that has completely healed him, as you can all see."

The journey has been difficult. But as I look back, I am amazed at how God has been with us and has gone before us every step of the way. And I am so thankful that He has allowed me more time with my husband, that my kids will enjoy more memories with their dad, and that our faith in God and love for each other has grown immensely through this time.

It is my prayer that as you read Travis' miraculous story of healing, you will remember that the same God that was with us in each and every moment, is the same God that is with you in whatever you face today. So, stand on His Word, hang on to His promises, and know that we are believing for *your* miracle!

In Him,

Natalie Hearn

PROLOGUE

I was in shock when I found myself face to face with the biggest trial of my life and was in desperate need of a miracle. My body was broken. My emotions were wrecked. My spirit was crushed. My state of mind was destroyed. And I was at rock bottom.

Maybe you can relate. Maybe you're facing your own trial right now. Maybe your situation is so big, so intimidating, so overwhelming, and so exhausting, that nothing short of a miracle is going to get you through.

If that's you today, I pray that after reading my story, you will see that your situation may be big, but our God is so much bigger. He is greater. He is stronger. He is more powerful. And there is nothing that He cannot do.

I pray that you will see that all things are possible. Your situation may look impossible, and in the human sense, it is. But not with God. With God, all things are possible. And He's going to see you through.

And most of all, I pray that you will see that there is always hope. There is hope for your healing. Hope for your heart. Hope for your mind. Hope for your relationship. Hope for your child. Hope for your freedom. Hope for your future. And there is not one situation or circumstance that God cannot fix, change, rebuild, reverse, overturn, or undo. He can do the miraculous. He can do things that are totally and completely unexplainable. I've seen it with my own eyes because He did it for me. And if He did it for me, I know that He can do it for you.

Chapter 1

COUNT IT ALL JOY

"Count it all joy, my brothers, when you meet trials
of various kinds..."
– James 1:2 (ESV)

Have you ever experienced a moment that immediately changed your life? A moment that came out of nowhere and totally blindsided you? A moment that took your entire world and flipped it upside down?

I've experienced some moments like that throughout my life. Moments that crushed me. Challenged me. Humbled me. Changed me. Moments that were painful, difficult, heavy.

But on Monday, November 14, 2022, I experienced a moment unlike anything I've ever been through before, and it completely changed my life.

This moment threatened my life, threatened my family, and threatened my future. It tried to attack my faith, steal my strength, and crush my hope. It shocked me, scared me, and shook me to my core. And the craziest part of all is that I never saw it coming.

———

When I woke up that morning, I had no idea what I was about to face. In fact, everything was going great. We had just come off of a record weekend at Impact Church, and I was on a high.

Three days earlier, on Friday, November 11th, Impact Worship had released our very first single titled "He is the Miracle" out into the world, and it began climbing the charts. Just two days later, on Sunday, November 13th, it had climbed to #1 on the iTunes Christian music chart, and #41 on iTunes across all genres. To say that we were ecstatic would be an understatement! We were totally and completely blown away by what God was doing through Impact Worship and Impact Church.

That same day, I preached a message to go along with the song's release. The message was also called "He is the Miracle," and it was all about how I believe that God is a God of miracles and how He still does modern-day miracles even today.

I shared about some of the many miracles of God throughout the Bible: how He parted the Red Sea and the Jordan River, how He spoke to Moses through a burning bush and Balaam through a donkey, and how He was with Shadrach, Meshach and Abednego in the fiery furnace and Daniel in the lion's den. I shared about how Jesus healed the sick, blind, deaf, mute, and lame, how He delivered the demon possessed, and how He raised dead people back to life.

And then I said this: "I've witnessed the countless miracles of God. And I want you to know that I believe that God can heal your body. He can restore, renew, and revive your marriage. He can reach your prodigal child. He can set the addict free. He can heal the brokenhearted. He can give you supernatural peace and joy. I believe He can turn your life a complete 180 because He did it for me. And if He can do it for me, He can do it for you because He is the miracle."

Little did I know that just 24 hours later I would be in desperate need of the very same kind of miracle that I had just preached about, and that everything that I believe in and teach on would be put to the ultimate test.

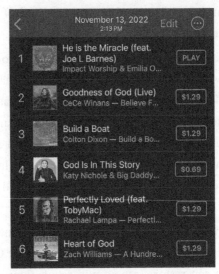

November 13, 2022, "He is the Miracle" reaches #1
on the iTunes Christian music chart

Mind blown that Impact Worship charted to number one on the
iTunes Christian music chart with our first song ever

By the time Monday morning arrived, I was a little tired from the weekend, but other than that, everything in my world was totally fine. Mondays are typically our day off, so my wife, Natalie, and I were hanging out and spending the day together, when we decided to go try a wellness therapy called a cold plunge.

The idea of a cold plunge is to submerge your body in a tub of freezing cold water for several minutes, and then enjoy the health benefits for hours to come. If you're thinking that this sounds totally miserable, I have to tell you, you're right. I had never been so cold in my life. In fact, it was downright painful. And as I sat in that tank, I decided that I would probably never try it again.

After the cold plunge, Natalie and I picked up our daughter, Jazzy, from school, and the three of us headed over to the church. Natalie had some work to catch up on, so the plan was to drop her off at the office for a bit while Jazzy and I ran to Target to do some shopping.

When we first got to the church and went inside, everything was totally normal...until we got back in the car. It was right about then, sometime around 3 p.m., that things started to change.

I had grabbed a handful of grapes on my way out the door, and as I sat in the car, I suddenly dropped one. Then another. And another. And before I knew it, I had dropped five grapes onto the floorboard of my car.

I thought it was kind of weird, but I chalked it up to the fact that we had just done that cold plunge a few hours earlier. I figured that it was probably some kind of side effect that was making my hands and fingers numb and that things would go back to normal in a few hours.

But then, a few minutes later, something else weird happened. Jazzy and I got to Target, walked inside, and I picked up my phone to text Natalie. But now, my right thumb wasn't doing what it normally did. It was numb. It felt heavy. And I wasn't able to type correctly.

I tried to explain it to Natalie over text, but as I typed, most of what appeared on the screen was a mess of jumbled up letters. I hit send, and within moments, Natalie was calling me. She spoke to me for just a few seconds and immediately knew that something was not right. She told me to go outside, get into my car, and wait there because she was coming to get me.

Now, here's what's crazy. The fact that Natalie even had a car with her was a miracle in itself. Normally, we drive both cars home from church on Sundays. But, for the first time in years, we had driven home together in my car the day before and left Natalie's car at church. The fact that she was able to leave and immediately get to me was a miracle and a sign of God's provision.

After Natalie picked us up, we went straight home. She wanted to call 9-1-1, but I really didn't want to. I was sure that if I laid down for a while, things would go back to normal. So, I convinced Natalie to let me rest for an hour, and I promised that if the numbness was still there when I woke up, I would go to the emergency room.

I had only been lying there for about five minutes when I realized that something wasn't right. I was about to go let Natalie know, but at the exact moment that I stood up, she was walking in to check on me. She took one look at me and she knew something was definitely wrong.

She immediately called 9-1-1 and said, "I think my husband is having a stroke." It was crazy to hear her say it because that wasn't at all on my radar screen. The thought had never even crossed my mind. At that moment, I was still stuck on the idea of the cold plunge.

The dispatcher told Natalie to have me lie on my back, and after I did, it felt like not even three minutes had passed before the paramedics arrived. It was seriously so fast and another miracle of God.

As they assessed me and checked things out, Natalie kept telling me that I needed to go with them in the ambulance to the ER, and I kept saying that I was fine and that she could just take me and drop me off. I did not want to ride in the ambulance to the ER.

But Natalie insisted. She told me "If I take you, you'll have to wait for hours. If you take the ambulance, you might get right in." I knew she had a good point. And thank God! Someone said, "There's something about a woman's intuition." And that's true! But there's also something about a Holy-Ghost-filled woman who is led by God. That's my wife, Natalie.

As I looked around the room full of firefighters and paramedics, I happened to make eye contact with one in particular. I decided to ask him what he thought I should do, and without hesitation he answered "Pastor, as a congregant of your church, I also think that you should take the ambulance in."

Can you believe that?

God is so good that He even sent me a messenger from my own church. I later found out that the paramedic's name was Ryan, and that he and his family had been attending Impact Church for the last two years. Yet another miracle!

The thing is, at this point, I only had two symptoms: I couldn't text and I couldn't hold on to grapes. That's it. I still had my thoughts, feeling, cognition, speech, and was otherwise totally normal. But the next thing I knew, I was on the stretcher and headed out to the ambulance. As they were wheeling me away, I was literally shouting to my family "It's OK guys!" and telling my wife and kids not to worry and that I would be fine.

But as soon as I got on that ambulance — BOOM. Everything hit. Hard. And I don't remember much after that.

I don't remember the drive over to the hospital at all, but I vaguely remember getting a CT scan, I vaguely remember getting stretchered to a helicopter, and I vaguely remember seeing my wife and Andre, the CFO and Executive Pastor of Impact Church (who is also one of my best friends), as I got onto that helicopter.

The one thing I do remember is Natalie giving me a kiss and taking a picture with me so she could show the kids. She didn't know if this would be the last time that she would see her husband. She didn't know if this was the last picture the kids would have.

Once I was loaded onto the helicopter, I was transported to a Level I trauma center. I don't remember the ride in the helicopter, I don't remember arriving at the trauma center, and I don't remember anything that happened next.

Later, my wife told me that after the helicopter landed, I was rushed inside to the emergency department where they immediately began running neurological tests on me.

They would do things like ask me to smile, ask me to lift both arms, ask me to lift both legs, and ask me to tell them how many fingers they were holding up. But I wasn't passing any of their tests.

They'd ask me to touch my nose, and I'd touch my chin. They'd show me pictures of things and ask me to describe them, and I couldn't do it. They'd ask me basic, simple questions, and I couldn't answer them.

When they asked me my name and my birthday, I didn't know. When they asked me what day it was and what year it was, I didn't know. When they asked me where I was, I didn't know. When they asked me my kid's names, I said "Forty."

I wasn't making any sense. I couldn't make my words. I was talking gibberish. And I was unable to communicate.

Then, Natalie said I got this sad and frustrated look on my face, and I started crying. I turned to look at her, and with tears in my eyes, I very clearly said "Count it all joy."

The doctor turned to Natalie and asked "What did he say?" He assumed that I was still mumbling nonsense. He had no idea that what I had just said was actually extremely significant.

But Natalie knew. She knew exactly what I had just said and exactly what it meant. She explained to the doctor that I was quoting scripture. And that what I had just said was actually a Bible verse from the book of James which says "Count it all joy, my brothers, when you meet trials of various kinds..." (James 1:2, ESV)

———————

Can you believe that?

I literally couldn't talk. I couldn't make a word out. I couldn't recall my own children's names (if you're a parent, try to imagine that one). But I could say as plain as day "Count it all joy."

This was yet another miracle of God, and a moment that He had prepared me for over 30 years earlier when I was in Bible school and had memorized the book of James by repeatedly reciting it aloud over and over again. Crazy.

The fact that He gave me the Scripture that I needed, when I needed it, how I needed it, and for what I needed it still blows me away today.

And I definitely needed it. Because not only was I in a trial, I was in the trial of all trials. And I was going to need to count it all joy.

Update from Erica to our Impact Church staff

Key Scripture:

"Count it all joy, my brothers, when you meet trials of various kinds..." James 1:2 (ESV)

Let's Pray:

Father, we know that You are sovereign, and that there is not one day, one hour, or one moment of our lives that is outside of Your power or outside of Your control. Today, I pray for those who are facing trials that have left them feeling shaken, unsettled, and insecure. God, I pray that as they stand firm on Your truths and hold tight to Your promises, they would be filled with peace knowing that You hold them securely in the palm of Your hand and You are in perfect control. We love you, Jesus. We pray this in Your mighty name, amen.

"As It Turned Out"

I was on shift with the Phoenix Fire Department when the call came in: there was a younger man, in his mid-forties, who was showing signs of a possible stroke. His main symptoms were slurred-type speech and an overall sense of not feeling right.

As we jumped into the truck and headed out on the call, I assumed that it would go like any other call, really. But that quickly changed once we arrived.

When we walked into the house, the first thing that I noticed was a Phoenix Suns sweatshirt and a beard. And the first thought that I had was that this guy kind of looked like my pastor. But as I got closer and saw Natalie standing there, I realized that this actually was my pastor and he might be in a bad spot.

I didn't say anything about knowing who he was. It didn't seem relevant to the situation, and I wanted to keep things professional. So, I just immediately went into work mode and got down to business as usual.

As paramedics on the firetruck, we take turns gathering information and getting everything entered into our system. And I really believe that God works in amazing ways, because as it turned out, it was my turn, and this would be my patient.

I began gathering Pastor Travis' information and medical history, and as I entered everything into our iPad, the rest of the crew got to work checking him out.

They checked his vital signs, his blood sugar, his blood pressure, his pupils, and his oxygen levels, but everything they checked was coming back great. There were no red flags, no obvious signs, and nothing made us think that he needed to be rushed to the hospital.

Next, the crew performed what we call a "stroke screen." They checked his grips, his mobility, and his strength. They asked him questions, talked to him, and assessed his responses. But again, he wasn't having any issues, in fact, he was checking out just fine.

It's crazy because, looking back, it is my belief that the devil was hiding and masking his symptoms. But I was very familiar with Pastor Travis. I knew what he normally sounded like. I knew his typical mannerisms. And there was something about his reactions, and even just the look on his face, that gave me the sense that something was not right.

After the evaluation was complete, we recommended that Pastor Travis go to the hospital to be checked out by a doctor, and when he agreed, we gave him the option of taking a car or the ambulance in. He asked Natalie what she thought he should do, and of course, she told him that he needed to take the ambulance, but he was still really hesitant to go.

There was some back-and-forth discussion, and then, there were about 30 seconds of silence. I remember it clearly because I had been pretty quiet for the entire call, but at some point during those 30 seconds, I suddenly had the feeling that I really wanted to talk to him.

My crew was still surrounding him as he lay on the floor, and as I walked around them and went to kneel down beside him, the movement must have caught his attention, because now, we were locking eyes, and he wanted to talk to me. He looked at me and asked me what I thought he should do, and without hesitation, I told him that I was a member of his church, he was my pastor, and I thought he needed to go in right now.

What struck me the most in this moment, and what really touched my heart, was Natalie's reaction. Because the second that I said it, I could feel her relief. The first thing she blurted out, and I'll never forget it, was "So, you know him and this isn't him." I remember looking at her and agreeing that yes, I did know him and this didn't feel like him. And I could tell she was just so relieved that there was someone else there who knew.

Finally, Pastor Travis agreed to take the ambulance in, and we immediately got to work getting him prepared. He still seemed to be doing fine, and he actually stood up and got onto our gurney with very little assistance. It wasn't until he was actually on the ambulance, about to leave, that I noticed his decline.

I had just finished up my report and transferred his care over to the next team of paramedics. The back of the ambulance was still open, and as I stood outside, I looked through the doors, looked right at him, and said "I'll be praying for you, Pastor." But he didn't react, and he didn't respond…it was almost like he was just not there.

I remember feeling a sense of urgency. I looked at the crew and told them to go, to just get moving. And after that, I got back in my truck, and I immediately started to pray.

Ryan Goettsch,

Firefighter/Paramedic, Phoenix Fire Department

Visiting Ryan at the firehouse almost two years after he responded to the 9-1-1 call that saved my life.

Scan here to listen to "He is the Miracle" by Impact Worship

"He is the Miracle" by Impact Worship

I've been broken
I've been let down
Haven't always felt You around
It is You I'm searching for
I will not find something more

When I seek I will find
When I knock You will open
When I seek I will find
When I knock You will open

You are the miracle
I've been waiting for
He is the miracle
I've been waiting on
Lift it up sing it out
Shout it loud
Let Him fill you up
You are the miracle
I've been waiting for

My heart longs for a beginning
Jesus You're in every ending
It is You I'm searching for
I will not find something more

When I seek I will find
When I knock You will open
When I seek I will find
When I knock You will open

You are the miracle
I've been waiting for
He is the miracle
I've been waiting on
Lift it up sing it out
Shout it loud
Let Him fill you up
You are the miracle
I've been waiting for

There is no one like You God
You are the only One
Father Spirit Son
There is no one like You God
You are the only One
Father Spirit Son

No one no one
No one no one

You are the miracle
I've been waiting for
He is the miracle
I've been waiting on
Lift it up sing it out
Shout it loud
Let Him fill you up
You are the miracle
I've been waiting for

Chapter 2

CLOSE IN CRISIS

"Yea, though I walk through the valley of the shadow of death,I will fear no evil; For You are with me; Your rod and Your staff, they comfort me."
– Psalm 23:4 (NKJV)

I really believe that you're never as close to Christ as when you're in the middle of a crisis. And that's exactly where I was after I was brought into the trauma center. I was in crisis. I was losing my speech. Losing my cognition. Losing control over the right side of my body. I was falling apart.

Doctors ran neurological tests on me all throughout the night. They came in every hour on the hour to check on me. They would check my peripheral vision. Ask me to perform tasks. Ask me questions.

Eventually, I was admitted to the ICU, and after a long and stressful night, we received life-changing news. I had suffered a hemorrhagic stroke. More specifically, a basal ganglia stroke. I found out later that 50 – 60 % of people who have a hemorrhagic stroke like this are likely to die. And doctor friends have told me that if you were going to have a stroke, a basal ganglia stroke is not the one you want to have.

The basal ganglia are located in the center part of the brain and connect all of the other parts of the brain together. They play a vital role in cognition, emotion, feeling, and most of all, speech. All things crucial in day-to-day life.

The news was shocking. I had no idea what was going to happen or what the outcome would be. I didn't know what this meant for my life, my future, or my family. All I knew was that I was in serious trouble, and I needed Jesus more than I ever had before.

———————

Maybe you've been there. Maybe you're even there right now. Maybe you're in the middle of your own health crisis, relational crisis, mental crisis, emotional crisis, or spiritual crisis. Maybe you're going through a crisis of fear, anxiety, worry, failure, shame, regret, betrayal, rejection or disease.

Whatever it is that you're going through today, I want you to know this. God is right there with you. He is close beside you. And He will not let you walk through your trial alone.

There are countless verses all throughout the Bible that talk about this. We know according to scripture that God will never leave us and never forsake us (Deuteronomy 31:6), that He is an ever-present help in times of trouble (Psalm 46:1), that He's a friend who sticks closer than a brother (Proverbs 18:24), that nothing can separate us from His love (Romans 8:38-39), and in Isaiah 7:14 we even read that Jesus Himself would be called Immanuel, which literally means "God is with us." How amazing is that?

———

Isaiah 43:2 (NLT) says "When you go through deep waters, I will be with you. When you go through rivers of difficulty, you will not drown. When you walk through the fire of oppression, you will not be burned up; the flames will not consume you."

I love this verse. It's such a powerful promise from God regarding His presence. And it really reminds me of the story of Shadrach, Meshach, and Abednego.

In Daniel chapter three, we read that these three young Hebrew men lived in Babylon when the king at that time, King Nebuchadnezzar, ordered the construction of a 90-foot-tall golden image. He then issued a decree that everyone must bow down and worship it. The law stated that if anyone didn't do this, they would be thrown into a fiery furnace and burned alive as punishment.

The Babylonians immediately began following the law. They

went along with culture, obeyed the decree, and bowed down to the golden image. But Shadrach, Meshach and Abednego wouldn't do it. They knew that they would be executed for disobeying, but they refused to bow down to anyone or anything but God.

This angered the king, so he had Shadrach, Meshach, and Abednego brought to him. He gave them one last chance to bow down before being thrown into the furnace, and still, they refused. They believed that God would save them from the fire and said "But even if he does not…we will not serve your gods or worship the image of gold…" (Daniel 3:18, NIV)

Now the king was furious. He ordered that the furnace be heated seven times hotter than normal, and then, he had his strongest soldiers come, tie the young men up, and throw them into the blazing furnace, fully clothed. The fire was so hot that as the soldiers approached, they were killed instantly by the flames, and Shadrach, Meshach, and Abednego fell into the fire.

The king was sitting there watching all of this happen, when suddenly, he looked at the furnace, jumped up and said, "Did we not cast three men bound into the midst of the fire? … I see four men loose, walking in the midst of the fire; and they are not hurt, and the form of the fourth is like the Son of God.'" (Daniel 3:24-25, NKJV)

WHAT. Did you catch that? The king sees four men walking around in the fire and he says that one looked like the Son of God. Do you know why it looked like the Son of God? Because it was! God was right there with them in the middle of it all.

Can you imagine? The fire was so hot that the guards were burned to death when they got too close, yet there Shadrach, Meshach, and Abednego were, just walking around with God inside of the flames.

And this next part is what really gets me. In Daniel 3:27 (NLT) we read "Then the high officers, officials, governors, and advisers crowded around them and saw that the fire had not touched them. Not a hair on their heads was singed, and their clothing was not scorched. They didn't even smell of smoke!"

I think that's such a cool detail that there was no smell. You and I know that when you get around a fire, you come away smelling like a fire. And yet, there was no evidence that these guys were ever even near one, let alone in one. There was no smell, no burns, no pain, no trauma, and no hurt. What a miracle!

———

The same thing happened with Daniel and the lion's den. You may be familiar with the story, but here's a little refresher if you're not.

In Daniel chapter six, we read about a godly young man named Daniel who worked as an administrator for the king. The Bible says that Daniel did such a great job and stood out so much from his colleagues, that the king made plans to place him over the entire empire.

This made his colleagues extremely jealous, and they immediately got to work trying to find fault with Daniel. But the more they looked, the less they found. In fact, Daniel 6:4 (NLT) says "...they couldn't find anything to criticize or condemn. He was faithful, always responsible, and completely trustworthy."

So, what did they do? They decided to try to get Daniel in trouble for worshipping God. They went before the king, convinced him to pass a law making it illegal to pray to anyone but him, and then, they turned Daniel in when he continued praying to God just as he always had.

The king was distressed when he found out about this. He did not want to punish Daniel. In fact, he spent the rest of the day trying to find a way to rescue him. But, because he had already signed everything into law, there was nothing the king could do.

That night, they took Daniel, threw him into the lion's den, and sealed the door with a stone. And when the next morning came, the king rushed back to check on him and was overjoyed to find that Daniel was still alive. Not only that, but when they pulled Daniel from the lion's den, we read in Daniel 6:23 (NLT) that "… Not a scratch was found on him, for he had trusted in his God." Sound familiar?

———

We tend to focus so much on praying that God would do the miracle of removing us from our trial completely. We want Him to get us out of our situation and out of our mess. And when it doesn't look like He's doing what we think He should be doing, we assume that He's not coming through.

But sometimes the miracle isn't in the removal of the trial. In fact, God may never take us out of it. The true miracle is that He's always with us in it. He covers us in it, goes with us through it, and He promises that we are never alone. And His presence changes everything.

———

I think that's one of the reasons that Psalm 23 is so popular. It's the most quoted, memorized, preached, and google-searched chapter in the Bible. And it's easy to see why. This passage is filled with hope for our hardest times, and it reminds us that God is with us.

In Psalm 23:1-4 (NKJV), David says:

¹The Lord *is* my shepherd;

I shall not want.

²He makes me to lie down in green pastures;

He leads me beside the still waters.

³He restores my soul;

He leads me in the paths of righteousness

For His name's sake.

⁴Yea, though I walk through the valley of the shadow of death,

I will fear no evil;

For You *are* with me;

Your rod and Your staff, they comfort me.

There are so many things that I love about this passage. It's full of layers. But today, I really want to focus on verse four because it's here that we see some very powerful and pointed language.

First, I love that David said *though* I walk, not *if* I walk. In other words, I'm going to go *through* some valleys.

And I like that he said *through* the valley and not *to* the valley. Because that's two entirely different locations. To the valley means that the valley is my final destination, but through the valley means that I'm just temporarily passing through. It means that there is another side, and there will be an end to this.

It's also significant that David referred to the valley as "the valley of the shadow of death." Because the shadow of death is not the same thing as the valley of death, and I love that he made that distinction. The valley of the shadow of death might look like death, feel like death, and seem like death, but the truth is, it's not death. It's just a shadow.

And yes, shadows can be scary. Yes, they can be extremely intimidating. But here are a few things that we happen to know about shadows: they always appear way bigger than reality, they've never actually hurt anybody, and they're not even real.

And I don't know if you've ever noticed, but anytime that I've ever seen a shadow, it's always been accompanied by a light. And what happens when you turn and look at that light? The shadow falls directly behind you.

Now check this out. In John 8:12 (NIV) Jesus said, "...I am the light of the world. Whoever follows me will never walk in darkness, but will have the light of life." Wow.

And that's exactly what David discovered.

Because if you look back at verses one through three, you'll notice that David started off using third-person language. He was talking about God. He said "the Lord is my shepherd... He makes me... He leads me... He restores me."

But then, when David began to talk about going through the valley, there was a powerful shift in his language. He stopped talking *about* God, started talking *to* God, and suddenly, his entire perspective changed. He said "I will fear no evil for You *are* with me."

I think that this change is very spiritually and biblically strategic. Because it's in the valleys of life where things start to get personal. Where religion turns to relationship. And where we come face to face with God.

A mature believer will tell you that the times they've been closest to God are the times that they've been in the valleys.

They enjoy the mountaintops, but they're thankful for the valleys because the valleys are what keep them close to Christ.

James 4:8 (NLT) says "Come close to God, and God will come close to you…" And Jeremiah 29:13 (NIV) says "You will seek me and find me when you seek me with all your heart." And it's really in the middle of our valleys where we tend to do just that.

Distractions are removed. We spend more time in prayer. More time in worship. More time in God's Word. More time in church. And the more we seek, the more we find that God is right there with us, and He's been there all along.

———

Something else I love about God is that He doesn't just go with us. When we read Deuteronomy 31:8, we discover that He actually goes before us.

Deuteronomy 31:8 (NIV) says "The Lord himself goes before you and will be with you; he will never leave you nor forsake you. Do not be afraid; do not be discouraged." Another translation says it like this … "for the Lord will personally go ahead of you."

I don't know about you, but I find it incredibly comforting to know that we have a personal God. And that there's not a place that we could go or a thing that we could go through, that He Himself hasn't already been.

It reminds me of when I was a kid, hanging out with my friends, and we would decide to do something scary. No matter what we were about to do, it always started out the same way. We would all look around, focus in on one friend in the group, and tell them "You go first."

If they did it and something went wrong, we would abandon the mission. But, if they did it and everything went OK, we would go ahead and do it too. There was something about having someone else go first that gave us the confidence and courage to move forward.

By the way, the adult version of this happens when you come home to find your garage door wide open. Has that ever happened to you? You know right away that you've either been robbed, or, you just left the door open. And it doesn't matter which thing may have happened, it always goes the same way at my house.

My wife looks at the house, looks at me, looks at the house again, and finally says … "You go first." So, I go in, go through the entire house, and check everything out. Then, I come back out and let her know that everything's good and she can come inside.

I love knowing that when it comes to my life, no matter what situation or fear I may face, God is right there saying "I'll go first." He's already gone where we're about to go. He's already next week, next month, and next year. He's already on the other side of everything that we face. And He says, "I'm already over here, I checked it out, and it's all right, you can come on through."

———

Psalm 139:7-12 (GNT) says "Where could I go to escape from you? Where could I get away from your presence? If I went up to heaven, you would be there; if I lay down in the world of the dead, you would be there. If I flew away beyond the east or lived in the farthest place in the west, you would be there to lead me, you would be there to help me. I could ask the darkness to hide me or the light around me to turn into night, but even darkness is not dark for you…"

I don't know what it is that you're facing today, but I do know that God is with you. He goes beside you and before you. There is no valley too deep, no crisis too dark, no fire too hot, and no trial too big to ever keep Him away.

We know through scripture that just like He was with David when he said "yea, though I walk through the valley," just like He was with Shadrach, Meshach and Abednego in the fiery furnace, just like He was with Daniel in the lion's den, and just like He was with countless others all throughout the Bible, He is with YOU. He has not left you. He never will. And He will always be close in crisis.

Key Scriptures:

"When you go through deep waters, I will be with you. When you go through rivers of difficulty, you will not drown. When you walk through the fire of oppression, you will not be burned up; the flames will not consume you." Isaiah 43:2 (NLT)

"Yea, though I walk through the valley of the shadow of death, I will fear no evil; For You *are* with me; Your rod and Your staff, they comfort me." Psalm 23:4 (NKJV)

"The Lord himself goes before you and will be with you; he will never leave you nor forsake you. Do not be afraid; do not be discouraged." Deuteronomy 31:8 (NIV)

Let's Pray:

Father, we thank you for the miracle of Your presence. We thank you that no matter what we're up against and no matter what we go through, we can hold on to Your promise that You will not let us face our trial alone. Today, I pray for those who are walking through the valley. I pray that as they look to You and keep their eyes on You, their fear would dissipate, their courage would rise, and they would move forward with confidence knowing that You are right there with them, you are close beside them, and Your presence changes everything. We love you, Jesus. We pray this in Your mighty name, amen.

Chapter 3

FAITH OVER FEAR

"By faith in the name of Jesus, this man whom you see and know was made strong. It is Jesus' name and the faith that comes through him that has completely healed him, as you can all see."

– Acts 3:16 (NIV)

After we learned that I had suffered a basal ganglia stroke, doctors pulled my wife aside and told her that she should prepare herself for the fact that I may never be the same again. They told her that of all of the places to have a brain aneurysm, this was the worst possible one. And then they said this: "the effects of a basal ganglia stroke are irreversible."

In other words, I was done. I would never be able to remember. I would never be able to comprehend. And I would never be able to communicate normally again.

When I look back now, I can't imagine how my family must have felt. I can't imagine what my wife went through hearing that her husband might not make it, and that if he did make it, he would never be the same.

I know that as Natalie heard those words, she was terrified. But do you know what else she was? She was strong and she was courageous.

She knew that in this situation we had two choices. We could listen to the doctors' words, and despair over how bad things seemed, or we could look to the Great Physician and declare His Word over our situation.

She decided right then and there that we weren't going to buy what an earthly expert told us, we were going to stand on what God's Word tells us. And God's Word tells us that our God is bigger and that it's already done.

So, on November 16, 2022, she made a post on her Instagram page, with a picture of us lying together in my hospital bed. The caption of the post said this: "By faith in the name of Jesus, this man whom you see and know was made strong. It is Jesus' name and the faith that comes through him that has completely healed him, as you can all see." (Acts 3:16, NIV)

That is so powerful and it still gives me chills to this day. She was holding fast to God's promises, holding fast to hope, and holding fast to truth, when it wasn't true yet.

Obviously, we were still afraid. It was a scary time. The future was unknown. My recovery was unknown. And anyone looking at the situation from the outside could see that things were not looking good. But I was alive. I was awake. I was still here. And we were ready to see what God was going to do.

We knew that we needed to let God bring me back, and we knew that He could do it. So, we were going to hold on to faith that He would.

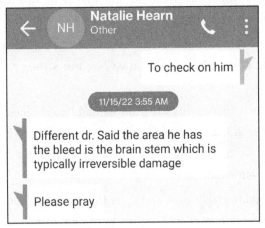

Natalie's update to Andre

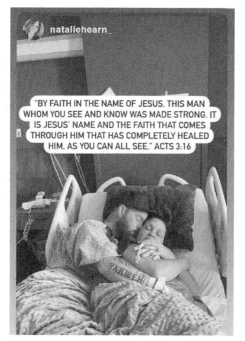

Natalie's Instagram story on November 16, 2022

It sounds so simple, to just have faith. Until we're faced with a situation where that's all that we can do. That's when we discover that for most of us, having faith can actually be really hard. We look around at our situation and our circumstances, and base our mindset on what we see, what it looks like, and how things seem.

If things aren't looking good, we decide that things must not be good. If the situation looks hopeless, we decide that it must be hopeless. If it looks like it's not going to work out, we decide that it's not going to work out. Even worse, we begin to live that way. We act and react as if it's already over.

And that's a big problem because our sight can fail us. It's not reliable. Our own understanding is not accurate. And we see things from a very limited human perspective.

2 Corinthians 5:7 (NIV) tells us "For we live by faith, not by sight." And that's a really important key to our victory when it comes to the trials of life.

When we live by faith and not by sight, we don't look at what we think we see, we listen to what we know God said.

If God said that He will make a way, then we believe that He will make a way. If He said that we can trust Him, then we believe that we can trust Him. If He said that He works all things out for good, then we believe that He'll work it out for good.

Things may not look good right now, but it doesn't matter how things look. We may not immediately see it in this moment, but it doesn't matter what we see. We take God at His word. We trust that He's a man of His word. And we have faith that He will keep His word.

———

The story of David and Goliath is such a great example of this.

The story begins in 1 Samuel 17 at the sight of an impending battle. The Israelite army is camped out on one side of a valley, the Philistine army is camped out on the other, and there's a battle line in between. But instead of marching forward to claim their victory, the Israelite soldiers are too terrified to even enter the fight. They're all paralyzed with fear over a Philistine giant named Goliath.

Goliath was over nine feet tall, wore 125 pounds of armor, and carried some serious weapons. And he wasn't just physically terrifying. He had a crazy attitude to match. Goliath loved to make a scene. The Bible says that he came to the edge of camp twice a day just to strut back and forth, taunt and mock the Israelite soldiers, and challenge them to fight.

One day, a teenage shepherd boy named David shows up to visit his brothers. He walks up to the battle line, hears Goliath taunting, and his reaction is totally different. He says "Who does that worthless Philistine think he is? He's making fun of the army of the living God!" (1 Samuel 17:26, CEV) And then he offers to take care of Goliath himself. Wow.

Isn't it amazing what a change of perspective can do? To the human eye, the situation didn't look promising at all. In fact, the Israelite soldiers were filled with fear every time they even thought about facing Goliath. But David wasn't looking at things from a human perspective. He was looking through the eyes of faith. He saw that the size of his problem was nothing compared to the size of his God, and he was filled with confidence and courage.

David later said in Psalm 42:11 (TLB) "But, O my soul, don't be discouraged. Don't be upset. Expect God to act! For I know that I shall again have plenty of reason to praise him for all that he will do. He is my help! He is my God!"

I love that! Expect God to act! Believe that He can bring you through. Believe that He will bring you through. And have faith until He does.

Moses is another great example of this. Did you know that the one thing that he feared the most was the very thing that God called him to go face?

Most of us know Moses as a biblical hero and one of the greatest leaders in the history of humanity. But before all of that, Moses' life situation was really just the opposite.

In Exodus chapter two, we read that when Moses was a young man, he killed an Egyptian and then tried to hide the evidence. Eventually, word got out about what he did, and when the Egyptian leader Pharaoh found out, he was so mad, he tried to kill Moses.

Moses ran from Pharaoh, went out into the desert to hide, and forty years later, guess what Moses was doing. He was *still* hiding in the desert.

One day, Moses is out, walking in the wilderness, when suddenly, a bush catches on fire, the voice of God speaks through the bush, and God tells Moses that he needs to go back to Egypt, and back to Pharaoh, because he has been chosen to lead the Israelites out of Egyptian bondage.

So, Moses is obedient to God, goes to Egypt, comes face to face with Pharaoh, demands the release of the enslaved Israelites, and then leads them out of Egypt and on toward the Promised Land.

Sounds pretty simple and easy when you read it like that. But the entire story is full of complications, situations, and tough circumstances where Moses demonstrated great faith over and over again.

Let me give you some examples.

When God first called him, Moses was freaked out by the entire thing. In fact, he was greatly insecure. He said this about himself in Exodus 3:11 (NLT) "Who am I to appear before Pharaoh? Who am I to lead the people of Israel out of Egypt?" And yet, in faith, he did as God commanded and went back to Egypt.

While he was in Egypt, he faced Pharaoh not just once, not just twice, but many times. In fact, God sent Moses to speak with Pharaoh at least ten different times before Pharaoh finally relented. Not only that, but each time Moses went before Pharaoh, God instructed him to perform signs to show Pharaoh that this was for real. And each time, Moses acted in faith, did as God instructed, and believed that God would show up and show out, just as He had promised.

And by the way, He totally did. Deuteronomy 34:10-12 (NIV) says this about Moses: "Since then, no prophet has risen in Israel like Moses, whom the Lord knew face to face, who did all those signs and wonders the Lord sent him to do in Egypt—to Pharaoh and to all his officials and to his whole land. For no one has ever shown the mighty power or performed the awesome deeds that Moses did in the sight of all Israel."

Another great example happened when the Israelites finally left Egypt. As they were on their way to freedom, Pharaoh had a change of heart, decided he wanted them back, and sent his entire army, complete with horses and chariots, to chase them down.

As the Israelites were fleeing from the army, they came up against a major roadblock...the Red Sea. There was no going forward, and no going back. They were trapped. And they were terrified.

To the human eye, it looked like it was over for the Israelites. But Moses wasn't looking through human eyes. He was looking through eyes of faith. And in Exodus 14:13-14 (NIV) we read that he told the people "Do not be afraid. Stand firm and you will see the deliverance the Lord will bring you today. The Egyptians you see today you will never see again. The Lord will fight for you; you need only to be still."

You may be familiar with what happened next – the Lord parted the Red Sea, the Israelites crossed over on dry land, and when the Egyptians tried to follow suit, they were thrown into confusion, the waters crashed down upon them, and they were swept into the sea.

One of the things I love about this story is the fact that Moses instructed the people not to be afraid. Because I'm sure that he was afraid. But Moses believed that God could do it. He believed that God would do it. And because he kept his faith in the face of fear, he was filled with confidence and courage.

———

2 Timothy 1:7 (NKJV) says "For God has not given us a spirit of fear, but of power and of love and of a sound mind." And I think that's such an important verse to remember when we face trials in life.

This verse isn't saying that we can't be afraid. In fact, if we didn't have fear, we wouldn't need faith. But there's a big difference between having a spirit of fear and being afraid. They're two radically different concepts.

We all have moments of being afraid. And when we walk by faith and not by sight, that's exactly what they remain. Moments. But when we have a spirit of fear, those moments take over our entire lives. Fear becomes what we're motivated and controlled by. And it has serious consequences.

A spirit of fear debilitates us. It discourages us. It dilutes our vision. It distorts our decision making. It limits us. And it steals our peace and our purpose.

And that's no way for a man or woman of God to live. God wants us to live a life of faith, to be filled with courage, and to do as David said and "Expect God to act!"

———

If you're in a situation today that has you filled with fear, if you're looking around, and based on what you see, things aren't looking good, it's time to stop looking at what you think you see and start listening to what you know God said.

God's Word says that He can do it: "Now all glory to God, who is able, through his mighty power at work within us, to accomplish infinitely more than we might ask or think." (Ephesians 3:20, NLT)

God's Word says that He will do it: "Let us hold unswervingly to the hope we profess, for he who promised is faithful." (Hebrews 10:23, NIV)

And God's Word says that it will probably be in a way that you never even thought of: "'My thoughts are nothing like your thoughts,' says the Lord. 'And my ways are far beyond anything you could imagine. For just as the heavens are higher than the earth, so my ways are higher than your ways and my thoughts higher than your thoughts.'" (Isaiah 55:8-9, NLT)

So let your faith rise up. Believe that God is going to act. Expect that He will do more than you expect. And have faith until He does!

Key Scriptures:

"By faith in the name of Jesus, this man whom you see and know was made strong. It is Jesus' name and the faith that comes through him that has completely healed him, as you can all see." Acts 3:16 (NIV)

"For we live by faith, not by sight." 2 Corinthians 5:7 (NIV)

"But, O my soul, don't be discouraged. Don't be upset. Expect God to act! For I know that I shall again have plenty of reason to praise him for all that he will do. He is my help! He is my God!" Psalm 42:11 (TLB)

"For God has not given us a spirit of fear, but of power and of love and of a sound mind." 2 Timothy 1:7 (NKJV)

Let's Pray:

Father, we thank You for Your Word that says that You have not given us a spirit of fear, but of power and of love and of a sound mind. Today, I pray against a spirit of fear, and I lift up those who have been living in its grip. God, I ask that You would make them strong. That You would make them courageous. And that as they lay their fears down at Your feet, a great faith would invade their hearts and be a powerful presence around them. We know that perfect love casts out all fear, and we're so grateful for Your perfect love today, God. We love you, Jesus. We pray this in Your mighty name, amen.

Chapter 4

A ROOM OF WORSHIP

"I praise God for what he has promised.
I trust in God, so why should I be afraid?
What can mere mortals do to me?"
– Psalm 56:4 (NLT)

As the days passed and my condition stabilized, my situation became clear. Now, I had total control of my left side, but not my right side. I could speak, but it was slow and slurred. My brain was working, but things were confusing and blurred.

Toward the end of the week, doctors and nurses started stopping by the room to tell us that this was miraculous and not normal. They told us that people go into comas after having this type of stroke, or they have no control at all over their limbs after having this type of stroke.

At this point, all I wanted was to worship and to hear worship music. And so, our hospital room became a room of worship and prayer.

Through slurred speech, I'd ask my family to play worship songs. I'd ask them to play our newest Impact Worship song, "He is the Miracle." I also don't think our next song release was a coincidence: "I Need Jesus."

So much of my time in the hospital is still really fuzzy for me, but I can clearly remember that right around this time, I think it was on day three or four, I was lying in bed, holding hands with some of my family members, when I had another song that popped into my head. It's called "Man of Your Word," and it's a song all about how God is a man of His word, and how He always keeps His word.

I remember thinking "God, I've preached everything that I know to preach for 30 years. I've told people that You're a man of Your word. I've taught that, I've preached that, and now I need you to show me that."

Our Impact Church worship leaders were there with us in the room, so I asked if they would sing that song, and as they began singing, everyone else in that hospital room began singing too. And do you know what I noticed?

As we sang about the goodness of God, all I could think about was the goodness of God. As we sang about the faithfulness of God, all I could think about was the faithfulness of God. And as we sang about the power of God, all I could think about was the power of God.

My situation didn't matter. My worries and my problems began fading away. And the more I focused on our great God, the more I was filled with hope, joy, peace, and faith.

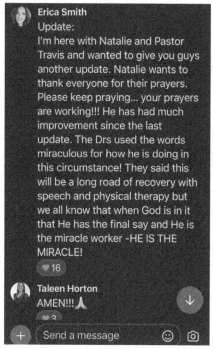

Erica Smith
Update:
I'm here with Natalie and Pastor Travis and wanted to give you guys another update. Natalie wants to thank everyone for their prayers. Please keep praying... your prayers are working!!! He has had much improvement since the last update. The Drs used the words miraculous for how he is doing in this circumstance! They said this will be a long road of recovery with speech and physical therapy but we all know that when God is in it that He has the final say and He is the miracle worker -HE IS THE MIRACLE!
♥ 16

Taleen Horton
AMEN!!! 🙏

Send a message

Update from Erica to our Impact Church staff

My daughter, Jazzlyn, and I together in the hospital

My son, Josiah, and my daughter, Kylie,
spending time with Dad in the hospital

There's a passage in the Bible that talks about this. It begins in Philippians 4:6-7 (NIV) where it says: "Do not be anxious about anything, but in every situation, by prayer and petition, with thanksgiving, present your requests to God. And the peace of God, which transcends all understanding, will guard your hearts and your minds in Christ Jesus."

The phrase "in every situation" really leaps off the page at me here. Because man, I was definitely in a situation. I couldn't think myself out of it, talk myself out of it, or get myself out of it. I was in a bad spot.

Chances are, you've been in a situation like that. In fact, almost everybody I know is currently going through a situation like that. I know people going through family situations, legal situations, health situations, financial situations, and every other kind of situation you can think of. Some of them are in situations that are so complicated, even their situations have situations. I've been there myself a time or two.

The passage goes on to say in Philippians 4:8 (NLT): "And now, dear brothers and sisters, one final thing. Fix your thoughts on what is true, and honorable, and right, and pure, and lovely, and admirable. Think about things that are excellent and worthy of praise."

I love those three words "fix your thoughts." Because that's exactly what worship does; it fixes our thoughts and focuses our thinking on God. When we worship, we think about who God is and what God can do. And when it comes to our trials and our situations, it makes a huge difference in the outcome.

———

When I worry, I fix my thoughts on me. I think about my problem, my fear, my situation, and my trial. And the more I worry, the worse things seem. That's because worry is a magnifier. It takes whatever problems we're worried about, and makes them seem even bigger.

It reminds me of a trip my family and I took to the mountains. From where we were staying, we had a beautiful view of a nearby mountain range, so one morning we decided to take a drive up into those mountains to go exploring.

As we were driving, I noticed that what had looked like a cool little mountain range from where we were staying, was actually much bigger. And the closer we got to these mountains, the bigger and more intimidating they seemed.

Did the mountains actually get bigger? Of course not. They were always the same size. It was our perspective that changed. We had surrounded ourselves with mountains, so mountains were all that we could see.

That's exactly how worries work. When we worry, we surround ourselves with fears, anxieties, concerns, and doubts. And so, all we can see are fears, anxieties, concerns, and doubts. And the more we worry…the more we worry, until we eventually end up filled with fear, paralyzed into inaction, and powerless.

———

That's what happened to Peter. In Matthew 14, we read that the disciples were out on a boat in the middle of the night when Jesus, who was back on shore, decided to go out and join them by walking out to them on top of the water. It was a dark and stormy night, and as He approached the boat, the disciples could see something coming, but they couldn't tell what it was and they were terrified.

Jesus called out, letting them know it was Him, but Peter wasn't convinced. He wanted Jesus to prove it by inviting Peter to walk on the water with Him. So, Jesus told Peter to come, Peter stepped out of the boat, and just like that, Peter was walking on water, too. What a miracle!

But then, Peter started looking around. He heard the wind, he saw the waves, and he became terrified and began to sink. He cried out for help, and Jesus responded by immediately reaching out to save him.

So...what happened? How did Peter go from walking on water one minute, to fearfully sinking the next? What happened to his faith and courage?

The key to it all is found in Matthew 14:30 (NLT). It says "But when he saw the strong wind and the waves, he was terrified and began to sink." Those first four words, "but when he saw," really sum up exactly what happened in this situation.

When Peter was focused on Jesus, when he was looking to Him, when he was listening to His voice, he was filled with courage to face his fears and step out of the boat in faith. And I love that because God's voice, the voice of our Father, really does bring encouragement, comfort, hope, and peace in the middle of our scary situations.

But, when Peter started looking at the wind and the waves, when he began to focus on his fears, his circumstances, his worries, and his doubts, that was when he became terrified and began to sink.

Now, do you want to see something really interesting? If we reverse a little bit to the beginning of the story, we see that just a few moments earlier, this exact same thing happened with all of the disciples.

When the story started out, the disciples were out on the water, hanging out in their boat, and things were totally fine. Until we read this in Matthew 14:26 (NLT): "When the disciples saw him walking on the water, they were terrified..."

Again, we see four words, "when the disciples saw." They were good until they saw something that scared them. It was only then that they became terrified.

In both of these instances, the same thing happened. They were influenced by their focus.

———

There's such power in where we put our minds, our thoughts, and our focus. In fact, Proverbs 4:23 (GNT) warns us that our entire lives are affected by this. It says "Be careful how you think; your life is shaped by your thoughts."

So, where should we put our thoughts? How do we stop focusing on what we don't want, and start focusing on what we do?

We read the answer earlier in Philippians 4:8 (NLT) when it said "...Fix your thoughts on what is true, and honorable, and right, and pure, and lovely, and admirable. Think about things that are excellent and worthy of praise."

I can't think of anything or anyone more true, honorable, right, pure, lovely, admirable, excellent, and worthy of praise than Jesus Christ, can you? When I take my focus off of me and put it on

Him, when I think about His power, His promises, His glory, His faithfulness, and His goodness, my outlook totally changes.

———

One of my favorite things to do every single weekend is to watch our church family worship and sing praises to God. That's because I can see people literally trading their worries for worship.

For some of us, praise and worship are the last things we think about doing when we're in the middle of a struggle. We're depleted, we're depressed, we're at rock bottom, and we just don't feel like we have anything left to give.

But the Bible tells us that this is exactly when we should be praising. In fact, Isaiah 61:3 (NKJV) says that for the spirit of heaviness, we are to put on "the garment of praise."

And the truth is, the deepest praise that we can give to God comes from a place of nothing. It comes from a place where God is our everything and our only thing. It comes when we finally realize that God is all that we need because He is literally all that we have.

———

Psalm 56:4 (NLT), says "I praise God for what he has promised. I trust in God, so why should I be afraid? What can mere mortals do to me?"

I love that it says "I praise God for what He has promised." Did you know that there are over 7,000 promises in the Bible for your life? Let me give you just a few examples.

God promises that:

He will strengthen you and help you (Isaiah 41:10)

He will fight for you (Exodus 14:14)

He will guide you (Psalm 32:8)

He will provide for you (Philippians 4:19)

He will protect you (Psalm 91:2)

He will give you wisdom (James 1:5)

He goes with you (Isaiah 43:2)

He goes before you (Deuteronomy 31:6)

He will never leave or forsake you (Deuteronomy 31:8)

He works things out for good (Romans 8:28)

He has a plan and a purpose for your life (Jeremiah 29:11)

And in 2 Corinthians 1:20 (NIV) we read that "no matter how many promises God has made, they are 'Yes' in Christ..."

In other words, God is a man of His word, and He always keeps His word. So, we can fix our thoughts on Him. We can remind ourselves of His promises. We can call them out. We can make them our prayer and our anthem. And we can thank Him in advance for fulfilling them.

———

I know that to the human mind, it seems counterintuitive to praise God when everything around you is falling apart, and to thank God for things that you haven't seen happen yet.

But here's the thing. Praise is a powerful spiritual weapon. It sets us free. It sets others free. And I've noticed that any big breakthrough is always preceded by praise.

Think about it.

The Israelites marched around the walls of Jericho for six days with no change. But on the seventh day, after they began to shout, blow trumpets, and praise, the walls of Jericho came crashing down and they were able to conquer the city.

Paul and Silas were stripped, severely beaten, and thrown into prison. But instead of despairing over their circumstances, they made the decision to praise. And after they began to worship and sing praises to God, the foundations of the prison were shaken, the prison doors flew open, and all of the prisoner's chains were loosed.

Moses was in the war of his life fighting against the Amalekites when he discovered this key to victory: the Israelites would win, but only if he kept his arms raised. Why were his raised arms so significant? Because raised arms are a symbol of praise.

Joseph was thrown into a pit and abandoned. He was as good as dead until one of his brothers, Judah, decided to come back and save him. It's interesting that out of all of his 11 brothers, it was Judah who came to his rescue. Why? Because if you were to look up the meaning of the word Judah, you would discover that the word Judah actually means praise.

Notice a theme here?

It was praise that broke down the walls of Jericho, praise that set Paul, Silas, and the prisoners free, praise that gave victory to the Israelites, praise that lifted Joseph out of the pit, and when we give God our worship and our praise, breakthroughs can happen in our lives too!

We recently released a song with Impact Worship called "When You Show Up," and in the lyrics, we sing "Worship till something happens, worship till your healing comes, worship till something changes…"

And that's exactly what happens when we worship. Things begin to change. Our worries get smaller as God gets bigger. Our faith rises. Our hope increases. Our trust deepens. And we're filled with joy, peace, and thankfulness.

———

When Jonah was in the belly of the whale, he said "When I had lost all hope, I turned my thoughts once more to the Lord…." (Jonah 2:7, TLB)

And if that's you today, if you've lost all hope and things aren't looking good, it's time to do the same.

It's time to take your focus off of your situation and put it onto your Savior. To trade your panic for praise and your worry for worship. And to fix your thoughts on who God is, what God can do, and what God has promised.

Remember. He is a good God. He is a faithful God. And He has not failed us yet.

Key Scriptures:

"And now, dear brothers and sisters, one final thing. Fix your thoughts on what is true, and honorable, and right, and pure, and lovely, and admirable. Think about things that are excellent and worthy of praise." Philippians 4:8 (NLT)

"Be careful how you think; your life is shaped by your thoughts." Proverbs 4:23 (GNT)

"… The oil of joy for mourning, The garment of praise for the spirit of heaviness…" Isaiah 61:3 (NKJV)

"I praise God for what he has promised. I trust in God, so why should I be afraid? What can mere mortals do to me?" Psalm 56:4 (NLT)

Let's Pray:

Father, help us to praise despite our circumstances and despite our situation. Help us to fix our thoughts on You, to focus our thinking on You, and to meditate on Your goodness, Your grace, Your kindness, Your mercy, Your love and Your faithfulness. Today, I pray for those who are feeling broken, those who are feeling low. I ask that You would give them the strength to praise anyway, and that as they begin to praise You, their spirit of heaviness would be lifted and they would experience joy. God, we praise You, we worship You, and we give You all the glory. We love you, Jesus. We pray this in Your mighty name, amen.

Scan here to listen to "When You Show Up" by Impact Worship

"When You Show Up" by Impact Worship

Lord I need You
I can't do this on my own
I believe You
Do the impossible

Do what only You can do
Come and move in me
Do what only You can do
Come and move in me

Lord I need You
I can't do this on my own
I believe You
Do the impossible
Do the impossible

Do what only You can do
Come and move in me
Do what only You can do
Come and move in me

When You show up miracles happen
When You show up fear is silenced
When You show up my faith is rising
When You show up

When You show up miracles happen
When You show up fear is silenced
When You show up my faith is rising
When You show up
Do whatever You wanna do

Lord I need You
I can't do this on my own
I believe You
Do the impossible
Do the impossible

Do what only You can do
Come and move in me
Do what only You can do
Come and move in me

When You show up miracles happen
When You show up fear is silenced
When You show up my faith is rising
When You show up

When You show up miracles happen
When You show up fear is silenced
When You show up my faith is rising
When You show up
Do whatever You wanna do

Do whatever You wanna do
Do whatever You wanna do
Do whatever You wanna do

Worship till something happens
Worship till your healing comes
Worship till something changes
He is here and He's ready to move

Worship till something happens
Worship till your healing comes
Worship till something changes
He is here and He's ready to move

Worship till something happens
Worship till your healing comes
Worship till something changes
He is here and He's ready to move
He is here

Worship till something happens
Worship till your healing comes
Worship till something changes
He is here and He's ready to move

He is here and He's ready to move
He is here and He's ready to move
And He's ready to move
He is ready to move

When You show up miracles happen
When You show up fear is silenced
When You show up my faith is rising
When You show up

When You show up miracles happen
When You show up fear is silenced
When You show up my faith is rising
When You show up
Do whatever You wanna do

Chapter5

STRENGTH IN THE STRUGGLE

"But he said to me, 'My grace is sufficient for you, for my power is made perfect in weakness.' Therefore, I will boast all the more gladly about my weaknesses, so that Christ's power may rest on me."
– 2 Corinthians 12:9 (NIV)

Finally, on November 18, 2022, the news came that they were ready to send me home. I was stable. I was no longer in any danger. And there was nothing more they could do for me there. It was time for me to get to work on recovering.

Let me tell you, I was so happy to be going home. Never take it for granted. But I also knew that my time in the hospital was only the beginning. I was about to walk out of one brutal battle, and step right into another.

My rehab and recovery would be a long and painful process. I would be going to multiple appointments per day, six days per week. I would have physical therapy, cognitive therapy, occupational therapy, speech therapy, and hyperbaric therapy. But I was already mentally, physically, and emotionally exhausted. And I knew that there was no way I was strong enough to do it on my own.

My message to our Impact Church staff - so happy to be going home

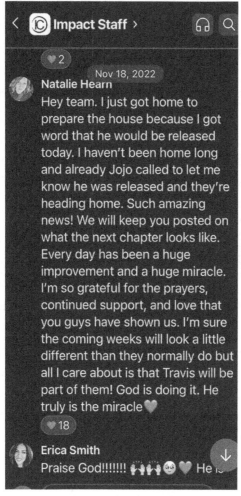

Natalie's update to our Impact Church staff

Have you ever felt like that? Just totally wiped out?

Life is like that sometimes. We get tired, weak, and weary. The weight of our trials wears us out and wears us down. We feel like our strength is gone and our power is gone. And eventually we get to the point where we consider giving up altogether.

I've noticed that it's usually in times like these when a well-meaning person tries to encourage us by saying, "What doesn't kill you makes you stronger." I don't know about you, but in those moments of life, I most definitely do not feel stronger.

But there's actually a very powerful, biblical truth to that saying because it's in our trials that God wants to be our strength. He wants us to lean on Him, depend on Him, and abide in Him, and He wants us to let Him carry us through.

There's a pretty well-known passage in the Bible that talks about this. I've preached on it many times because it has really spoken to me throughout my life, and it continues to do so today.

In 2 Corinthians 12:7-10 (NIV), Paul says, "...Therefore, in order to keep me from becoming conceited, I was given a thorn in my flesh, a messenger of Satan, to torment me. Three times I pleaded with the Lord to take it away from me. But he said to me, 'My grace is sufficient for you, for my power is made perfect in weakness.' Therefore I will boast all the more gladly about my weaknesses, so that Christ's power may rest on me. That is why, for Christ's sake, I delight in weaknesses, in insults, in hardships, in persecutions, in difficulties. For when I am weak, then I am strong."

There's a lot to unpack in this passage, so let's break it down a little bit.

It starts out with Paul saying that he has a thorn in his flesh. He never tells us exactly what the thorn is, but I like how he leaves it wide open like that because then we can all identify with it. We all know what it's like to have a thorn.

A thorn simply represents a hurt or a pain. It's something that irritates, bothers, and torments us. And it just does not seem to go away.

It might be an emotional pain, a mental pain, a relational pain, or a physical pain. It might be something that's noticeable to others, but most of the time, we deal with it silently and nobody ever really knows about it but us.

Paul also tells us something very important about his thorn. He calls it "a messenger from Satan." That's because Paul knows that the problem that he's facing is not really the true problem. It goes much deeper than that. He knows that there is a spiritual war taking place in this world, and that his thorn is really an attack by Hell.

That means that Satan may have initiated it, but God is allowing it. Why? Because God always has a purpose in pain. And He specializes in taking what the enemy intended for evil and turning it for good.

Paul goes on to say, "Three times I pleaded with the Lord to take it away from me." This part is so crazy to me because three times seems really, really light. I've pleaded with the Lord many times to remove some of the thorns in my life, and I'm pretty sure that in my desperation, I've asked more than three times within a single sentence. The fact that Paul asked three times total just blows my mind.

But I love God's response to Paul. He says "my grace is sufficient for you, for my power is made perfect in weakness."

Notice that God doesn't say anything about removing Paul's thorn. He doesn't say anything about fixing Paul's problem. Instead,

He says His grace is sufficient. In other words, Paul, I'm not taking it away because you need it in your life. But I will cover you in My grace, and fill you with My power, so that you'll be OK.

Finally, Paul says "That is why, for Christ's sake, I delight in weaknesses, in insults, in hardships, in persecutions, in difficulties. For when I am weak, then I am strong."

It sounds like such a contradiction. That you can be weak and at the same time be strong. And in the human sense, it is. But Matthew 19:26 (NIV) tells us "With man this is impossible, but with God all things are possible."

———

Just one chapter before this in 2 Corinthians 11:23-27 (NIV) Paul wrote:

"Are they servants of Christ? (I am out of my mind to talk like this.) I am more. I have worked much harder, been in prison more frequently, been flogged more severely, and been exposed to death again and again. Five times I received from the Jews the forty lashes minus one. Three times I was beaten with rods, once I was pelted with stones, three times I was shipwrecked, I spent a night and a day in the open sea, I have been constantly on the move. I have been in danger from rivers, in danger from bandits, in danger from my fellow Jews, in danger from Gentiles; in danger in the city, in danger in the country, in danger at sea; and in danger from false believers. I have labored and toiled and have often gone without sleep; I have known hunger and thirst and have often gone without food; I have been cold and naked."

At first glance, it might seem like Paul was griping, complaining, or maybe even bragging about his problems. I know some people like that. They brag about all that they've been through.

But that's not at all what Paul was doing. Paul wasn't sharing this so that we would know what he had been through, he was sharing it so that we would know what God had brought him through.

That's why Paul says he delights in weakness. Paul knows that it's in his weakest moments that God can display His sovereign power. And when Paul talks about being strong, he isn't talking about standing on his own strength. He's talking about standing on the strength of the Almighty God.

———————

It's amazing what a human can do when they have the power of God living inside of them.

It reminds me of a story in the Bible about a guy named Samson. In the book of Judges, we read that Samson had a reputation for being a really strong dude. He killed a lion with his bare hands. He singlehandedly took on 1,000 Philistines in a fight and won. I mean, this guy's reputation was just crazy.

Now, if you grew up in church and went to Sunday school, or if you've ever read a kid's Bible, you've probably read the story of Samson and remember him being depicted as this big muscleman type of guy.

But here's what's really interesting. In Judges 16:6 (NLT) we read "So Delilah said to Samson, 'Please tell me what makes you so strong and what it would take to tie you up securely.'"

Delilah asking Samson where his strength comes from tells us something really important, and that's that the answer probably wasn't that apparent. It wasn't that obvious. And the physique that we see him depicted with in little kid's books and Bible stories, was probably not his actual physique.

And I love that because it shows that sometimes our greatest strength is invisible. It doesn't come from us. When on the outside, it looks like there's no way we should have as much strength as we do, we can be strong because our strength comes from the quietness and power of the Holy Spirit of God in our lives.

———

We tend to think of strength in terms of how much we can accomplish or get through on our own. But nowhere in the Bible does it tell us to be strong in our own strength. Instead, it says "…be strong in the Lord, and in the power of his might." (Ephesians 6:10, KJV)

The Bible talks a lot about this. Here are just a few examples:

"He gives strength to the weary and increases the power of the weak." Isaiah 40:29 (NIV)

"Don't be afraid, for I am with you. Don't be discouraged, for I am your God. I will strengthen you and help you. I will hold you up with my victorious right hand." Isaiah 41:10 (NLT)

"My flesh and my heart may fail, but God is the strength of my heart and my portion forever." Psalm 73:26 (NIV)

"The Lord God is my strength…" Habakkuk 3:19 (NKJV)

"The Lord is my strength and my song…" Exodus 15:2 (NLT)

"…for the joy of the Lord is your strength." Nehemiah 8:10 (NIV)

"For I can do everything through Christ, who gives me strength." Philippians 4:13 (NLT)

"'Not by might nor by power, but by my Spirit,' says the Lord Almighty." Zechariah 4:6 (NIV)

These verses are saying that God can give us strength. He can give us power. And when we feel broken and weary, it's a good place to be in because when we are weak, He is strong.

I love this example from Paul in 2 Corinthians 4:8-9 (NIV). He says "We are hard pressed on every side, but not crushed; perplexed, but not in despair; persecuted, but not abandoned; struck down, but not destroyed."

In other words, I'm pressed, I'm getting the squeeze of my life, but I'm not crushed. You can attack me, target me, come at me all you want. But I'm God's property, and when I'm God's property, I have God's power.

———

I don't know what it is that you're going through today, but I do know that we're all going through something. And when our strength is gone, our power is gone, and we feel like giving up, there is an answer to our weakness and that answer is the strength of Jesus Christ.

It doesn't matter what inadequacies, insecurities, or weaknesses we might be going through; He is stronger than our struggles. He is more powerful than our problems. And the same promise that He gave to Paul, is the very same promise that He gives to us today: "My grace is sufficient for you, for my power is made perfect in weakness." (2 Corinthians 12:9, NIV)

I've experienced firsthand that we can be at the weakest moment of our entire lives, we can be broken, wrecked, dissipated, and destroyed, and that's when God shows up and says let me show you how strong I can be through you. I've experienced that even when the situation is dire and things seem impossible, "With men it is impossible, but not with God; for with God all things are possible." (Mark 10:27, NKJV)

The Bible never said it would be easy, but the reality is, God will not only give us the strength to make it through, He will flip the script, demonstrate His power in our weakness, and take what the enemy meant for evil and use it for good.

So, when you're weak, trust in Him, depend on His strength for your life, and let Him use your pain for His purpose. Remember that when you are weak, He is strong! And He will give you the power and strength that you need to make it through!

———

Key Scriptures:

"My grace is sufficient for you, for my power is made perfect in weakness." 2 Corinthians 12:9 (NIV)

"Finally, my brethren, be strong in the Lord, and in the power of his might." Ephesians 6:10 (KJV)

"For I can do everything through Christ, who gives me strength." Philippians 4:13 (NLT)

"'Not by might nor by power, but by my Spirit,' says the Lord Almighty." Zechariah 4:6 (NIV)

Let's Pray:

Father, we know that true strength and true power come from You. And that when we're too weak to make it on our own, we can trust You to carry us through. Today, I lift up those who feel depleted, tired, broken, weak and weary. I pray that as they lean on You, depend on You, and abide in You, they would discover that Your grace is sufficient, and that nothing is impossible with You. We know that when we are weak, You are strong, God, and we ask You to be our strength today. We love You, Jesus. We pray this in Your mighty name, amen.

Chapter 6

FIRST ONE IN, LAST ONE OUT

"Bear one another's burdens, and so fulfill
the law of Christ"
– Galatians 6:2 (NKJV)

One of the things that really stands out to me about this entire period of time is the huge amount of love and support that I was shown. From the night that I was taken away by ambulance, to my time in the hospital, to my release back home and the months that followed, there was not one single moment where my family and I had to walk through this fire alone.

When I was stretchered out of the house, my wife Natalie reached out to our good friend Erica for help, and within minutes Erica was pulling into our driveway, ready to take Natalie to the hospital. She showed up for us, and continued to show up for us, stepping in and helping in any way that she could.

When my daughter Kylie received the call that I had suffered a stroke, she immediately jumped on a flight and left San Diego in the middle of the night. She rushed to Phoenix to be with me, and it meant everything to have her by my side.

When I was in the hospital, friends and family members filled my room to overflowing. They were there all day, every day, sitting with us, comforting us, encouraging us, and spending hours with us in that hospital until eventually, my wife had to kick them out so that I could rest.

When I got out of the hospital, I received thousands of handwritten letters that the church had collected while I was gone. People wrote personal notes. They sent offers of help. They shared prayers and scriptures. And they showed so much empathy, sympathy, and love.

One of the notes that I received was from Maricopa County Sheriff Paul Penzone. He's a part of the Impact Church family, and it was so special to me because he not only came and spent several hours with me, he also wrote me a poem. How powerful is that?

I had pastors from around the world, pastors I had never met or even spoken to before, reaching out to let me know that they had heard my story, and that they, their staff and their church were praying for me.

I heard from old friends, new friends, people I was surprised to hear from, and people I didn't even know were still alive. There were just so many people who called me, texted me, and sent messages to show me love and support.

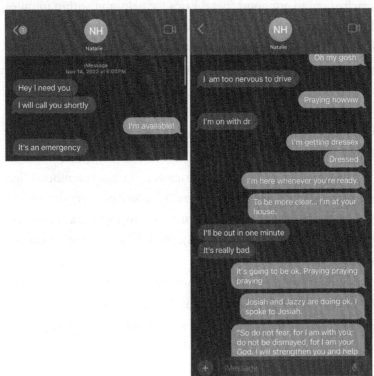

Text conversation between Natalie and Erica the night of my stroke

---

One moment that I'll never forget happened just a week after I got out of the hospital. I was at home with my family, hanging out, and we had just finished watching the Suns game. My phone rang, and when I looked down at the screen, I was surprised to see an incoming FaceTime call from Phoenix Suns head coach Monty Williams.

I figured it was a mistake and that he must have dialed me on accident as the game had literally just ended, but I answered the call just in case, and when it connected, there was Coach Monty on the screen with the entire coaching staff standing behind him. They had called to let me know that they were praying for me, and to see how I was doing.

I visited with them for a minute, and then Coach Monty told me to hold on because he had some more people there who wanted to talk to me. And as he walked to the other side of the locker room and turned the screen, there was the entire team. It was so good to see their faces.

I actually took a screenshot during that call, and in it you can see Coach Monty, Deandre Ayton, Chris Paul, Mikal Bridges, Cam Johnson, Cam Payne, Damion Lee, and Devin Booker.

But what really strikes me about that day is they didn't just text me. And they didn't just call me. They went out of their way to FaceTime me, and they made sure to do it with everyone. They took the time to get together, right after their game, to show me love and to let me know that they cared. And it meant the world to me.

FaceTime call with Coach Monty and the Suns -
so good to see their faces

I was so blessed, and still am so blessed, to have had such an incredible support system. And thinking about scripture, that's really what life is about. That's why Ecclesiastes 4:12 (GNT) says "Two people can resist an attack that would defeat one person alone…" and Galatians 6:2 (NKJV) tells us to "Bear one another's burdens, and so fulfill the law of Christ."

These verses are saying that we're not meant to go through the fires and trials of life alone. We are better together. We are stronger together. And we are made to lift each other up, encourage each other, support each other, and help each other to fight.

There's a story about Moses in Exodus 17 that I really think is such a perfect depiction of this. In the story, we read that there's a battle going on between the Israelites and the Amalekites, and Moses is watching it all from the top of a nearby hill.

Each time that Moses raises his arms and keeps them raised, the Israelites are able to advance on the Amalekites. But each time that he gets tired and lowers his arms, the Amalekites begin to overtake them. This goes on for so long that Moses becomes exhausted. His arms begin to give out, his legs begin to get weak, and his body becomes extremely fatigued.

But check this out. Moses' brother Aaron and his nephew Hur were right there with him, and they immediately jumped in to offer their support. They put a rock under him so he could sit down, they stood on either side of him and held up his arms, and they stayed that way until the sun went down and the Israelites received their victory.

I get goosebumps just thinking about that story, because that really is exactly what I felt. I had so many Aarons and Hurs in my life. And I never could have done it without them.

There's absolutely no way that I could have fought this battle on my own. There's no way that my wife could have fought this battle on her own. And I am overwhelmed with emotion and gratitude for everyone that fought for me and still continues to fight for me to this day. The whole experience has taught me, and really inspired me, to want to be there for others and do the same.

There are too many men and women of God who want from God, but don't want to do anything for God or for people. They see a problem, or see someone in need of help, and because it's not their problem, and it's not their issue, they brush it aside and go on with their lives and on with their day.

But listen. If God let us see it, it's now our problem. If God put it in our path, it's now our problem. And as men and women of God, we need to step up, step in, and take action.

Jesus gave us a great example of this in the parable of the Good Samaritan. In Luke 10:30-35 (NIV) we read:

"A man was going down from Jerusalem to Jericho, when he was attacked by robbers. They stripped him of his clothes, beat him and went away, leaving him half dead. A priest happened to be going down the same road, and when he saw the man, he passed by on the other side. So too, a Levite, when he came to the place and saw him, passed by on the other side. But a Samaritan, as he traveled, came where the man was; and when he saw him, he took pity on him. He went to him and bandaged his wounds, pouring on oil and wine. Then he put the man on his own donkey, brought him to an inn and took care of him. The next day he took out two denarii and gave them to the innkeeper. 'Look after him,' he said, 'and when I return, I will reimburse you for any extra expense you may have.'"

There are so many things about this story that really stand out to me:

First, it says that the man was walking from Jerusalem to Jericho when he was attacked. And that's really the way that life seems to go. It's when you're minding your own business, not looking for trouble, just trying to get through the day, that the enemy suddenly attacks.

Next, it says that he was stripped of his clothes. And it's crazy because that's exactly what the enemy does. He strips you of all hope, strips you of all faith, strips you of all peace, strips you of all joy, and he tries to rob you of every good thing that God created for you.

Finally, it says that he was beaten and left half dead. This part of the story really hits deep, because that was literally me after I had my stroke. In fact, a month or so after I was released from the hospital, my wife and I went to the doctor for a follow-up visit and he told me that I was incredibly lucky because I should be "dead or a vegetable." So, reading that this man was half dead, I can definitely relate.

Now here's where I want us to really pay attention.

The Bible says that first, a religious leader walked by, saw the man, saw the problem, and instead of doing something to help, he crossed the road and passed by on the other side. A little while later, another person walked by, saw the man, saw the problem, and did the same. It's crazy because they both saw the problem, and they both looked it off like it wasn't their problem. Have you ever done that? I know I have.

But then, the Good Samaritan came through and he was the game changer. He stepped up, stepped in, and did all that he could to help. He saw the need and he filled the need. And because of him, the man's life was saved.

I love this story so much. And it reminds me of the many, many Good Samaritans that I had in my life after my stroke.

One that comes to mind immediately is Dr. Ashley. She's a doctor of physical therapy who specializes in neurology, and she also goes to our church. The moment that she heard about the stroke, she messaged me on Instagram, introduced herself, and said that she wanted to help. And then she proceeded to give the next six months of her life to my healing.

Another member of our church, Caleb, is the owner of a gym called Glory Gains. After hearing about my stroke, he reached out to let me know that after I graduated and advanced out of physical therapy, he would like to help me get my health on track by offering my family and I free memberships, and free training, for life.

I have countless stories like that, and I experienced an overwhelming amount of support. People showed up, showed out, and took care of things before I could even ask for help, and in many cases, before I even realized I needed it.

And that really is the key. Not just that we show concern and sympathy for others, but that we actually do something with it. That we see a need, and then jump in to fill the need, no hesitation and no questions asked.

My physical therapist, Dr. Ashley, and I

Caleb and I at Glory Gains Gym

The truth is that very few people do this. They want to walk with you when life is good: when the money's good, when the favor's good, when the blessing's good, when the association's good, but they don't want to walk with you when you're going through a fire.

But as men and women of God, we should never let anyone go through a fire alone. It is our job and our responsibility to show up for people when they need us the most. And our presence and our willingness to fight can make all the difference in the world.

——————

It reminds me of when I was a kid and I saw my first housefire. I vividly remember standing outside and watching as this house in my neighborhood burned to the ground.

But the thing that stood out to me the most wasn't the actual fire. It wasn't the flames shooting into the sky or the black billowing smoke. What captivated my attention, and the thing that I still clearly remember to this day, was the firefighters.

The moment that they showed up everything changed. Their presence alone was powerful. It shifted the entire atmosphere. It was incredible to watch as they fearlessly rushed into the house, and ran straight into the fire, to rescue anyone who was stuck in the blaze.

And they didn't come into the situation unprepared. They were covered in protective gear. They wore coats, pants, helmets, hoods, gloves and boots, all designed to protect them from the heat, smoke and flames.

I later learned that this gear is called "turnouts," and that really is the perfect description and illustration of what we should do when we see people going through fires around us. When the heat turns up, we need to turn out and show up as spiritual firefighters, armored up and ready to rescue them from the flames!

—————

It reminds me of Ephesians 6:13 (NIV) which says "Therefore put on the full armor of God, so that when the day of evil comes, you may be able to stand your ground, and after you have done everything, to stand."

This passage is saying that wearing the right armor and protection is just as important in a spiritual battle as it is in a physical one. And when we jump in to fight spiritual fires, we had better come prepared.

A few verses later in Ephesians 6:18 (NIV), we read "And pray in the Spirit on all occasions with all kinds of prayers and requests. With this in mind, be alert and always keep on praying for all the Lord's people." And I really want to focus on this for a minute because it's extremely important.

When it comes to life's fires, prayer is the first thing, and really the only thing, that we need to do. It's a powerful spiritual weapon. It moves the hand of God. And it not only helps us fight our battles, it's what helps us win.

When I was in the hospital, I had so many people just covering me in prayer. I could never name or list them all if I tried. My friends prayed. My family prayed. My church family prayed. Our staff prayed. And I will never forget waking up in the ICU, opening my eyes, and seeing our friend Pastor Toni just warring for me in prayer in the back corner of the room.

James 5:15-16a (KJV) says "And the prayer of faith shall save the sick, and the Lord shall raise him up; and if he have committed sins, they shall be forgiven him. Confess your faults one to another, and pray one for another, that ye may be healed..."

I think that this is one of the most powerful verses on prayer. And I honestly believe that's why I'm here today. My life is the result of men and women from around the world, praying earnestly for my healing.

The passage goes on to say that "The effectual fervent prayer of a righteous man availeth much." (James 5:16b, KJV)

In other words, prayer changes things. It makes things happen. It gets results. And when we show up for someone in the middle of a fire, it's the most powerful and effective thing we can do.

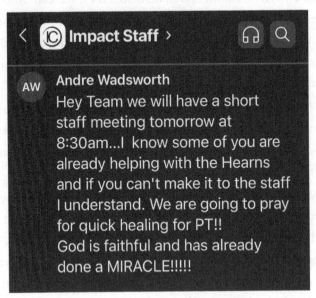

Andre's message to our Impact Church staff calling for a meeting to pray

One of the mottos for firefighters is "first one in, last one out." I love that so much! And it's exactly what I want us to do as spiritual firefighters.

Let's be the first ones in and the last ones out. Let's show up and show out for people when they need us the most. Let's war for them in prayer. Let's stand by their side and fight. And let's be people who stick it out and see them through to the very end.

I know that it's not going to be easy, but people need us. Their lives depend on us. So, let's treat this like the rescue mission that it is!

Key Scriptures:

"Bear one another's burdens, and so fulfill the law of Christ." Galatians 6:2 (NKJV)

"Two people can resist an attack that would defeat one person alone. A rope made of three cords is hard to break." Ecclesiastes 4:12 (GNT)

"And pray in the Spirit on all occasions with all kinds of prayers and requests. With this in mind, be alert and always keep on praying for all the Lord's people." Ephesians 6:18 (NIV)

"And the prayer of faith shall save the sick, and the Lord shall raise him up; and if he have committed sins, they shall be forgiven him. Confess your faults one to another, and pray one for another, that ye may be healed. The effectual fervent prayer of a righteous man availeth much." James 5:15-16 (KJV)

Let's Pray:

Father, Your Word instructs us to "bear one another's burdens, and so fulfill the law of Christ," and we ask that You would help us to do that today. Open our eyes to the needs of those around us, and help us to be people of courage and action, men and women of God who show up, show out, and fearlessly run into fires to fight for people when they need us the most. And for those who are in the middle of their own battles, attacks, or fires today, God, send them Aarons and Hurs, Good Samaritans, and spiritual firefighters to stand with them, lift them up, encourage them, support them, and help them to fight. We know that we serve a good God, and we are grateful. We love You, Jesus. We pray this in Your mighty name, amen.

"Overcome" by Paul Penzone

Right now it may feel like you're broken and beat,
Your body feels fragile, you fear of defeat

Your faith has been tested, you're overwhelmed by the fear,
A setback has rocked you, the future's unclear

There is no rhyme and no reason, no warning, no sign,
You've never strayed from His path, His will is divine

It's not His hand nor His punishment, He only gives you His love
Every blessing and every trial are His plan from above

It is times like these you'll see the tears on His face,
He cries for your suffering, He extends you His grace

Your path to recovery may feel too long to endure,
Yet, it's your faith and His love that provide you the cure

First One in, Last One Out

I know right now the road seems rocky and long,
Just trust in His plan, be patient, be strong

He will heal your body, He will show you the way,
His plan for the next stage will become more clear with each
day

God has blessed you with the gifts He keeps special for some,
You were chosen for divine purpose, you will overcome.

Chapter 7

A SECOND CHANCE

"What a God we have! And how fortunate we are to have
him, this Father of our Master Jesus! Because Jesus was
raised from the dead, we've been given a brand-new
life and have everything to live for, including a future in
heaven—and the future starts now!"
– 1 Peter 1:3-5 (MSG)

Have you ever been given another chance? Maybe you were a kid and got in trouble and your mom gave you another chance. Or maybe in a relationship or a job, you messed up but you were given another chance. If that's ever happened to you, then you know the feeling. Relieved. Grateful. Thankful. Blessed.

That's how I was feeling when I made it home from the hospital. And that's how I still feel as I write this today. I was overwhelmed with gratitude and just could not believe that God had given me another chance at life.

I was so ready to start the process of recovery. I wanted nothing more than to heal and feel normal again. So as soon as I could, I started putting in major work. My life became rehab on rehab on rehab, and I was doing non-stop training and therapy.

———

I went to hyperbaric therapy, red light therapy, and EMF therapy, and I worked with my physical therapist, Dr. Ashley, on rebuilding my strength. She would come to the house and run me all around the neighborhood. She would come to the church and run me up and down the halls. She had me lifting weights, performing exercises, and dragging her around with resistance bands. And she made sure I was working out every single day.

With my speech therapist, I worked a lot on speaking and enunciation. At every appointment, she would hand me a sheet of at least 20 tongue twisters and have me repeat them over and over again. It was actually really amazing because eventually, she asked if I would like to practice my preaching instead.

At cognitive therapy, my therapist would hold up a series of flashcards with pictures on them and have me describe what I saw on each one. The pictures were of a variety of different things, and some were really hard for me to name. One week, she showed me a picture of a volcano. I knew in my mind what it was, but all I could think of was "lava fire."

Another week, she showed me a picture of a sea horse, and I could not think of the word no matter how hard I tried. I finally looked at my her and said, "This is gonna sound crazy, but all I can come up with is water horse." And we both started laughing.

At occupational therapy, we worked a lot on motor skills and regaining what I had lost on my right side. We did a lot of strength exercises, coordination exercises, squeeze exercises, and hand bike exercises, but one of the biggest things we worked on was feeling.

My therapist had this big bowl of rice with a bunch of small hidden objects inside. She would have me close my eyes, pull out the objects one at a time, and identify them without ever opening my eyes. I pulled out things like beans, pennies, paperclips, and nails, but it was really hard to figure out what they were because I couldn't feel them.

I also practiced daily to relearn how to type. Before the stroke, I was really fast at typing and could type as fast as I talked. But now, my hand was totally numb and I just couldn't do it.

I remember sitting in the doctor's office, taking a typing test, and being devastated to learn that my results were 20 words per minute. The doctor was really happy with it, and said that I had done a great job, but I sat there at the keyboard and just started to weep.

I knew there was no way that I could do what I do without being able to type at my normal speed. Typing was a skill that I used daily, and without it, there was no way I would be able to write my sermons.

Therapy was a long, hard road, and at times I was pretty discouraged. I'm not ashamed to admit that on more than one occasion, I left my appointments and cried. But over time, and with lots of work, I was slowly improving.

I started gaining my speech back. My memory back. My cognition back. My strength back.

And I was getting better and better, and stronger and stronger every single day.

I still had lots of work to do, but the way I saw it was that God truly is the miracle. He is the God of second chances and new beginnings. And I just could not believe that He gave me a do-over at life.

Putting in major work at therapy

The word "do-over" really reminds me of when I was a middle school athlete, and I used to go out and play pickup basketball with my friends. There is one thing I remember very distinctly about playing sports in middle school. If you made a mistake when you were playing, you could say one thing … "do-over." And for some reason, everyone was totally fine with it. Your mess up would be forgotten, you would be given a second chance, and things would restart as if nothing had ever happened.

Now, once you got to high school, it was a totally different situation. You could forget the idea of having a do-over ever again. If you messed up, that was just too bad. You had to suck it up, pull yourself together, and keep on going.

I've noticed that many of us tend to live our lives the same way. For some reason, when things aren't going as we hoped, or when we mess up or make a mistake, we think that it's over. We believe that we're stuck in our situation, stuck in our sin, stuck in our mess, and it's too late for things to ever change. We assume that because this is the way it is, this is just the way it has to be. But nothing could be further from the truth.

With God, a do-over is always possible. It doesn't matter what your current situation is or how you got into it. He is a God of grace, mercy, new life, new hearts, and fresh starts. And He is so good that He keeps on giving them over and over again.

———

The Bible talks a lot about this. It's full of stories of God giving second chances, do-overs, and brand-new beginnings.

Let me give you a few examples:

We all know Moses as the man who led the Israelites out

of Egypt and to the Promised Land. But before that, he lost his temper, killed someone, fled Egypt, and was hiding out in a foreign land.

Jonah was headed in the complete opposite direction of where he was supposed to be. So, God used a storm to stop him in his tracks and get him on the path to his purpose.

Esther was an orphan. She felt alone, abandoned, and forgotten. But one day Esther became queen and God used her to save Israel.

Job lost everything he had, including his health, wealth, and family. But God blessed the second half of his life even more than the beginning, and gave him back double of everything he ever had.

David committed adultery, got the woman pregnant, and had the husband killed. The whole situation basically fell apart. And yet, after David repented, God restored his life, used him in mighty ways, and called him "a man after my own heart."

Joseph saved two nations from famine and became second in command of all of Egypt. But before that, he was sold into slavery and sentenced to prison.

Rahab was a prostitute. Yet after she helped the Israelite spies, she gave her life to Christ, got married, had children, and in Matthew chapter one, we read her name in the family line of Jesus Christ.

Paul, also known as Saul, hated Christians and had them killed. Until the day God struck him blind. Three days later his sight was restored, his life was changed, and he went on to light the world on fire for Jesus.

All of these stories and all of these people have one big thing in common. God used their trials, dark times, difficult moments, and hard places to prepare them for and propel them to their future.

———

It may not feel like it in the moment, but sometimes a trial really is the best place we can be. It's in our trials, when we've hit rock bottom, that most of us finally start to look up. It's in our pain and our problems, that we finally start to pray. And it's in our hard times, that we finally put our mind on Christ.

David wrote about this in Psalm 119:71-72 (NLT) when he said "My suffering was good for me, for it taught me to pay attention to your decrees. Your instructions are more valuable to me than millions in gold and silver."

———

We tend to falsely believe that because God loves us so much, He would never let us go through any pain. But the truth is, He loves us so much that He does allow pain in our lives to get us where He wants us to be. And sometimes, He's got to break us to remake us, stop us to give us a new start, and give us an ending in order to make room for a brand-new beginning.

One of my favorite examples of this is in a vision that God gave to the prophet Jeremiah. The story is found in Jeremiah 18:1-4 (NLT) and in it we read:

"The Lord gave another message to Jeremiah. He said, 'Go down to the potter's shop, and I will speak to you there.' So I did as he told me and found the potter working at his wheel. But the jar he was making did not turn out as he had hoped, so he crushed it into a lump of clay again and started over."

This passage speaks so loudly to me because of the phrase "didn't turn out as he hoped."

Sometimes, that's the way life goes. It just doesn't turn out like we hoped. I know I've felt that way before.

Have you?

Maybe your marriage didn't turn out as you hoped. Or your health didn't turn out as you hoped. Or your career didn't turn out as you hoped. Or maybe even you didn't turn out as you hoped.

Next it says that the potter "crushed it into a lump of clay again." Oftentimes, when things don't turn out as we hoped, we feel crushed. Our plans are crushed. Our future is crushed. Our dreams are crushed. Our relationship is crushed. Our hearts, minds, and spirits are crushed.

But listen to this next part. Right after Jeremiah saw this, the Lord said to him "…As the clay is in the potter's hand, so are you in my hand." (Jeremiah 18:6, NLT) God is saying that we're the clay, and He's the potter. And that means that if you're crushed today, you are in His hands. He is remolding, reshaping, and rebuilding you. And He's not done with you yet.

―――――――

King Solomon, the wisest man on earth, said in Proverbs 20:30 (GNT) "Sometimes it takes a painful experience to make us change our ways." And that's really how we need to think about our trials … they're a God-given opportunity to change.

Think about it.

A health trial is usually what it takes to motivate us to work out, eat right, take better care of ourselves, and finally get healthy.

A relational or emotional trial might be the final straw in getting us to finally decide to go to rehab, to counseling, to anger management, or to work on our mental health.

A spiritual trial will move us to finally give our lives to Christ, find a church, join a small group, and spend time in God's Word and in prayer.

A financial trial will force us to really get serious about our money, to stop spending, to start saving, and to develop new financial habits.

These types of trials are painful. We don't want to go through them. But they also offer us opportunities to do things differently. To work on ourselves. To rebuild. To recommit. To reinvent. And to do some things that we never even knew were possible.

———

That's been one of the greatest blessings for me. I've had so many opportunities to experience change. And because of that, I have a brand-new outlook on life. I see things from a new perspective, and I look at things through a totally different lens, than I did before. And I am just so grateful for another shot. I'm so thankful for another chance at being a husband, a daddy, and a good pastor to my church family. And I will never take it for granted.

One thing about my personality is this: I'm an all or nothing type guy. And I've been given another chance so... that means I'm going into this thing full on. I'm going to take advantage and maximize every new opportunity that God gives me: spiritually, emotionally, relationally, and physically. And I'm just getting started.

1 Peter 1:3-5 (MSG) says "What a God we have! And how fortunate we are to have him, this Father of our Master Jesus! Because Jesus was raised from the dead, we've been given a brand-new life and have everything to live for, including a future in heaven—and the future starts now!"

I love that! And if you're in a trial today, I want that to really sink in…. "we've been given a brand-new life and have everything to live for … the future starts now."

Your trial is not the end. God is the God of fresh starts, do-overs, and brand-new beginnings. And He can give you another chance!

Key Scriptures:

"What a God we have! And how fortunate we are to have him, this Father of our Master Jesus! Because Jesus was raised from the dead, we've been given a brand-new life and have everything to live for, including a future in heaven—and the future starts now!" 1 Peter 1:3-5 (MSG)

"The Lord gave another message to Jeremiah. He said, 'Go down to the potter's shop, and I will speak to you there.' So I did as he told me and found the potter working at his wheel. But the jar he was making did not turn out as he had hoped, so he crushed it into a lump of clay again and started over." Jeremiah 18:1-4 (NLT)

"Sometimes it takes a painful experience to make us change our ways." Proverbs 20:30 (GNT)

Let's Pray:

Father, we thank You for fresh starts, do-overs, and brand-new beginnings. We know that we're not perfect, but we serve a God Who is, and we're so grateful that You love us so much that You're willing to give us chance after chance, and keep on working on us, no matter how long it takes. Today, I lift up those who are feeling broken and crushed. We know from scripture that you are close to the brokenhearted and that you save the crushed in spirit, and I pray that they would feel Your closeness and Your presence today. Remind them that You see their heart and You see their situation, and that You can take what's broken and crushed and rebuild it to wholeness once again. We love You, Jesus. We pray this in Your mighty name, amen.

Chapter 8

WHY IS THIS HAPPENING TO ME?

"My dear friends, do not be surprised at the painful test
you are suffering, as though something unusual were
happening to you. Rather be glad that you are sharing
Christ's sufferings, so that you may be full of joy
when his glory is revealed."
– 1 Peter 4:12-13 (GNT)

I've noticed that no matter what kind of trial we're facing, and no matter what the circumstance is, we all tend to have one thing in common when these moments come. We all ask the same question...

Why is this happening to me?

I know I did. I was totally shocked and confused when doctors told me that I had suffered a stroke. I mean, I had zero health problems. I don't drink, smoke or do drugs. I don't take any kind of medication for anything. I don't think I've ever even had a cavity.

I had zero warning, and I showed no symptoms and no signs. In fact, the week before the stroke happened, I was in the middle of the application process to update my life insurance and I had received an A+ rating. Yet four days later...I almost died.

So...why?

I've heard this question a lot in my years of ministry. It's a totally normal question to ask when your world is falling apart around you. And an explanation might even make things a little easier to endure. But the truth is, when it comes to our trials, we may never know the exact reasons for each one that we face, at least not in this life.

The one thing we do know is this. Jesus told us in John 16:33 (NLT) "...Here on earth you will have many trials and sorrows..." So, if you're a human and you live on planet Earth, trials are a guarantee.

The Bible talks a lot about this. It warns us over and over again that we will face trials, and there are three main metaphors that we often see used when it comes to talking about hardships.

We see the idea of storms.

In the storms of life, it feels like problems are raining down, issues are raining down, worries are raining down, and we're about to drown in troubles. We're hit by crashing wave after crashing wave, and we just can't seem to catch a break.

We see the idea of valleys.

In the valleys of life, things are dark and quiet. It seems like nobody is with us, nobody understands us, and nobody gets what we're going through. We feel isolated, alone, and desperate, and we can't see a way to make it to the other side.

And we see the idea of fires.

In the fires of life, we enter a process of refining that Isaiah 48:10 (NLT) compares to the "furnace of suffering." And that's exactly what it feels like. It's painful and personal. It's filled with adversity and affliction. And just when we think we can't take anymore, the heat gets turned up even hotter and we're thrown right back into the middle all over again.

We tend to have the misconception that good people should or will avoid hard times. But Jesus never promised that any of us would have a pain-free life, in fact, He said the opposite. Matthew 5:45 (NLT) says "...For he gives his sunlight to both the evil and the good, and he sends rain on the just and the unjust alike."

That means that good things happen to bad people and bad things happen to good people. Even Jesus himself, who was sinless and the epitome of good, was murdered by capital punishment and nailed to the cross.

And in 1 Peter 4:12-13 (GNT) we read "My dear friends, do not be surprised at the painful test you are suffering, as though something unusual were happening to you. Rather be glad that you are sharing Christ's sufferings, so that you may be full of joy when his glory is revealed."

Did you catch that? It says, "Do not be surprised…as though something unusual were happening." For some reason, I'm still surprised when I go through things in life. But this verse is telling us that not only are trials to be expected, they're actually very normal and common.

The fact is, life is not fair. It will never be fair. And we should never expect it to be fair. We live in a fallen world, and because this is Earth and not Heaven, we are going to experience many different types of pain.

———

Now, here's the thing with trials. Just because they're going to happen, doesn't mean that every single one of them has to happen. As humans, we tend to put ourselves through a lot of unnecessary pain as a result of our own foolish actions and decisions.

That's exactly what happened to Jonah. In the first verse of the book of Jonah, we read that God told Jonah, a Hebrew prophet, to go to the city of Nineveh to preach against it because of its wickedness.

The people of Nineveh had a terrible reputation. In fact, they were known to torture and kill anybody that loved God. And Jonah was so terrified at the thought of facing them, that he responded by running away and jumping on a ship headed in the other direction.

During the voyage, God sent a terrible storm that threatened to break the ship apart. And as the crew desperately tried to figure out what to do about it, Jonah had a realization. He told the sailors "Throw me into the sea ... and it will become calm again. I know that this terrible storm is all my fault." (Jonah 1:12, NLT)

Most of us remember what happened next. Jonah was thrown overboard, swallowed by a whale, and spent three days and three nights inside of it until he was finally spit out onto dry land. And after all of that, guess where Jonah eventually ended up... Nineveh.

So, how did this happen to Jonah? Why did this happen?

In this case, the answer is clear. The reason for the trial was Jonah. God told him exactly what to do, and Jonah did the opposite. If he would have just listened to God, he would have never even been on that ship in the first place. But because of Jonah's disobedience, he suffered, and so did everyone around him. Every person on that ship went through a terrible storm, all because of Jonah.

I've noticed that we tend to act a lot like Jonah in our own lives. We ignore what God's Word says and do what we want instead. We put ourselves in bad places, bad situations, bad relationships, and bad circumstances. And then we wonder how we ended up in the middle of a storm. Even worse, we blame it all on God and ask Him why He did this to us.

But just like Jonah, the reason for our trial is us. We made bad decision after bad decision and it finally caught up with us. Not only that, we dragged everyone around us into our situation, and they too had to pay the consequences.

If this is all sounding just a little too familiar, then what happened to Jonah should really encourage you. Because even after he sinned, ran from God, created a huge mess of his life, and found himself at the bottom of the sea, his story didn't end there. In fact, it was just beginning. Because God showed up, rescued Jonah, and gave him a second chance. Jonah still went to Nineveh, he still preached God's Word, and he still fulfilled God's plan and purpose for his life.

And if God did it for Jonah, He can do it for you. It doesn't matter what your situation is. It doesn't matter why it's happening. It doesn't matter how you got here, how long you've been here, or how bad things may seem. There is nothing too dark, no place too deep, and no person too far gone for God.

———

Now, let's talk about a totally different kind of trial. The kind of trial that comes out of nowhere. It has no visible explanation. We didn't do anything to get ourselves here. In fact, it's just the opposite. We thought we were doing everything right. We were doing our best, making good choices and good decisions, and we still ended up in a mess.

That's exactly what happened to Job. Job had it all: health, wealth, and happiness. He had a wife and ten children. He had thousands of livestock, sheep, oxen, and cattle. He definitely had it going on.

Not only that, but Job was a good man. He was a really good man. In fact, God said this about him in Job 1:8 (NIV) "...There is no one on earth like him; he is blameless and upright, a man who fears God and shuns evil."

But one day, the devil started messing with him, and all of a sudden, Job started losing it all. His kids died. His animals died. His land was destroyed. He got a life-threatening disease. He lost everything he had, just like that.

To top it all off, Job's friends went ahead and added insult to injury by suggesting to Job that maybe it was all his fault. They said that he must have brought this upon himself by sinning.

Job wasn't just in a major trial; he was in multiple major trials. And listen to how he responded. The Bible says he fell to the ground in worship and said "...Naked I came from my mother's womb, And naked shall I return there. The Lord gave, and the Lord has taken away; Blessed be the name of the Lord." (Job 1:21, NKJV) Wow.

So, did Job get himself into this? Did he create his own mess? The answer is obviously no. Job 1:8 tells us that Job was doing everything right. We know that this happened because the enemy was attacking Job. God allowed it to happen, but He didn't cause it. And neither did Job.

One of the things that I really love about the story of Job is the way that it ends. Because after everything that Job went through, God didn't leave him there. Just like He did with Jonah, God showed up, rescued him, and gave him another chance. God restored Job's health, restored his life, and blessed him back with double of everything that he ever had. And in Job 42:12 (NLT) we read "So the LORD blessed Job in the second half of his life even more than in the beginning..."

I think some of us really need to hear that today. We might be in the lowest of the lows. Our trial might be so dark and so painful that we've lost all hope for the future. But this trial is not the end.

Our best days are not behind us. And God can make our second half even better than our first.

Jeremiah 29:11 (NIV) says "'For I know the plans I have for you,' declares the Lord, 'plans to prosper you and not to harm you, plans to give you hope and a future.'" God has plans after this trial. Not just a plan. But plans. Spiritual plans. Emotional Plans. Physical plans. Eternal plans. Plans for hope and a future!

Hebrews 13:8 (NLT) tells us "Jesus Christ is the same yesterday, today, and forever." That means that the same God who rescued Jonah, the same God who restored Job, and the same God we read about all throughout the Bible, is the same God with us in our trials today. He has the same love, the same care, the same ability, the same power, and the same presence when it comes to us. And He can work in and through our trials just like He did with them.

I have definitely felt that. I've been worn down, crushed, and discouraged. I have experienced pain and problems I never imagined I would face. But through it all, I've seen God do the miraculous. I've seen Him work in situations that seemed impossible. I've seen Him do things that are totally and completely unexplainable. And I've experienced the mighty hand of God on my life in ways that I never have before.

Key Scriptures:

"My dear friends, do not be surprised at the painful test you are suffering, as though something unusual were happening to you. Rather be glad that you are sharing Christ's sufferings, so that you may be full of joy when his glory is revealed." 1 Peter 4:12-13 (GNT)

"I have told you all this so that you may have peace in me. Here on earth you will have many trials and sorrows. But take heart, because I have overcome the world." John 16:33 (NLT)

"'For I know the plans I have for you,' declares the Lord, 'plans to prosper you and not to harm you, plans to give you hope and a future.'" Jeremiah 29:11 (NIV)

Let's Pray:

Father, we thank You that You see us and You see our situation. We're so grateful that there is not one trial, valley, storm or fire in our lives that ever takes You by surprise. Today, I pray for those who are facing an unexpected trial. I ask that You would fill them with Your peace. That even though their world is shaken around them, they would experience a deep and supernatural peace within them. Help them to put their faith in You, knowing that they can trust You with their situation, and they can trust You with their outcome. We love You, Jesus. We pray this in Your mighty name, amen.

Chapter 9

THIS IS WAR

"Stay alert! Watch out for your great enemy, the devil.
He prowls around like a roaring lion, looking for
someone to devour."
– 1 Peter 5:8 (NLT)

Now, I want to talk some more about the question "why is this happening to me?" Because if there's one lesson that I learned in 2022, it's that spiritual warfare is no joke.

It's no coincidence that the very same weekend that we released our first worship song into the world, the very same weekend that our song went number one and defied all odds, and the very same weekend that I preached a message titled "He is the Miracle," was the very same weekend that I would suffer a brain aneurysm and hemorrhagic stroke.

No. This wasn't a coincidence at all. This was personal. It was an attempted assassination by the devil himself, a demonic attack against me and my family. And no one could ever convince me otherwise.

———

The truth is, there is a constant spiritual battle taking place in this world, and we are in an all-out war. In fact, if you could put spiritual goggles on, and look into the spirit realm, what you would see would blow your mind.

There are right now, at this very moment, angels and demons battling it out over you because the enemy is after your soul, your salvation, your joy, your peace, your comfort, your purpose, your sanity, your mental health, your spiritual health, your emotional health, your physical health, and anything else he can get his hands on.

Have you ever heard the expression that someone is "battling their demons?" It's crazy because that's not just a saying, it's a reality. And most people have no idea just how true it is.

Ephesians 6:12 (NIV) says "For our struggle is not against flesh and blood, but against the rulers, against the authorities, against the powers of this dark world and against the spiritual forces of evil in the heavenly realms."

I've noticed that these days, we all seem to be warring against each other. We think that the problem is our spouse, our neighbor, our coworker, our community, and people who don't think like, act like, or see things like us.

But this verse is saying that our battle is not against another person or group of people that God created in His very own image. The real battle is against "the rulers, against the authorities, against the powers of this dark world and against the spiritual forces of evil in the heavenly realms."

In other words, our battle is against Satan, his demons, and the powers of Hell. And this is a spiritual fight.

Now, I don't like to give the devil too much attention, but if you don't understand your enemy, he can and will destroy you. So, I think it's important that we talk about his true intentions.

John 10:10 (NIV) says "The thief comes only to steal and kill and destroy..." And that's exactly what his intentions are with you. He has no other goals, no other agenda, and no other ideas.

His sole purpose is to take you down, take you out, and destroy everything and everyone around you in the process.

And he's not waiting on a formal invitation to do it. In fact, the Bible warns us that it's just the opposite. 1 Peter 5:8 (NLT) says "Stay alert! Watch out for your great enemy, the devil. He prowls around like a roaring lion, looking for someone to devour." Another translation of this same verse says he is "seeking whom he can devour."

In other words, be ready and watch your back. Because the devil is out, he's looking around, and he's planning to attack.

———————

Ephesians 6:16 (NLT) says "In addition to all of these, hold up the shield of faith to stop the fiery arrows of the devil." And I think that's such a powerful illustration of what the devil does. He shoots arrow after arrow, and launches attack after attack, just waiting for something to land.

He shoots arrows of depression and anxiety. He shoots arrows of guilt and shame. He shoots arrows of fear and failure. He shoots arrows of doubt and insecurity. He shoots arrows of betrayal and regret. He shoots arrows of sickness and disease. He shoots arrows of loneliness and despair. And he just keeps on shooting.

But here's the thing.

Isaiah 54:17 (NKJV) says that "No weapon formed against you shall prosper..."

That means no depression or anxiety, no guilt or shame, no fear or failure, no doubt or insecurity, no betrayal or regret, no sickness or disease, no loneliness or despair... NO WEAPON!

The devil can shoot all the flaming arrows he has at you. He can design and assign every evil scheme he can come up with. And he can attack you all he wants. But no weapon formed against you shall prosper!

The devil may try to convince you that there's no hope, but you and I know that the devil is a liar and the truth is not in him, because the truth, which is God's Word, tells us that there is always hope.

He may try to steal from you. He may come after your joy, peace, kindness, love, character, name, integrity, or reputation. But let's just say he was successful in all of that. Let's say he took the whole world from you. He still can't take the Jesus inside you, and he can't steal your salvation.

He may try to take all of your freedom. He may try to lock you up and imprison you, even within your own mind. But he's not the giver of freedom, Jesus is, and the Bible says "where the Spirit of the Lord is, there is liberty." (2 Corinthians 3:17, NKJV)

If he can't defeat you, he's going to try to discourage you. If he can't destroy you, he's going to try to put you in despair. If he can't win, and by the way, he knows he can't win, he's going to try to wear you down and wear you out.

But Romans 8:31 (ESV) says "What then shall we say to these things? If God is for us, who can be against us?" Romans 8:37 (NIV) tells us "No, in all these things we are more than conquerors through him who loved us." And in 1 John 4:4 (ESV) we read "... he who is in you is greater than he who is in the world."

In other words, when you have the spirit of God Almighty within you, it doesn't matter if all of the spiritual forces of evil surround you. God is greater, stronger, and more powerful. And the attacks of the enemy simply won't work.

Maybe you really needed that reminder today. Maybe you've been under attack, you've been dealt some serious blows, and it feels like the devil has been working overtime in your life. Maybe you're even at the point where you feel like giving up.

Psalm 27:14 (MSG) says "Stay with God! Take heart. Don't quit. I'll say it again: Stay with God."

One thing I've learned about spiritual warfare is that the battle is always the hardest right before the breakthrough. And what the devil throws at you shows what's in you. So, if you feel like all of Hell is gunning for you and you're being hit from every direction, I want to encourage you today...stay with God and do not quit.

The devil knows that your breakthrough is coming. So he's throwing every last thing he's got at you. But keep going. Keep fighting. Keep pressing. Your victory is right around the corner. So do not give up and do not quit!

I've definitely taken some hits. The devil took his best sucker punch at me, he threw his best shot at me, and he went all in on his attempt to take me down and take me out.

But do you know what? I'm still here. I'm still standing. And I will not quit.

My message to our Impact Church staff -
still struggling but determined to fight back

He tried to take my health, my cognition, my speech, and my memory away. But I will not quit.

He tried to take my wife's husband, my children's daddy, and my church's pastor away. But I will not quit.

He tried to take my calling, my preaching, and my teaching away. But I will not quit.

He tried to take my handwriting, my typing, my singing, and my songwriting away. But I will not quit.

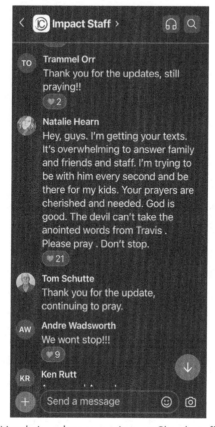

Natalie's update to our Impact Church staff

He tried to shut me down. He tried to shut me up. But I want everyone to know that the devil will never shut me up. If I had to babble about Jesus, if I had to mumble about Jesus, I can't be shut up and I will not quit.

I will not back down. I will not slow down. I will not give in. I will not give up. And I will not quit. Because this is war...and I'm here to fight.

The first few weeks after I had my stroke, I was really fighting for my mental health. I was tired and worn out. I was down and depressed. I was crying all the time. And I was not in a good place mentally.

But I'm so thankful for the power of a woman of God in my life. Because Natalie not only had such a heart for me in the dark place that I was in, she also knew exactly what it would take to pull me out.

She knew that worship is a powerful spiritual weapon, and that for the spirit of heaviness, we are to put on "the garment of praise." She kept telling me "Trav, you should go write songs and go worship God. I think it would be really good for you."

So, just nine days after my stroke, and just a few days after I got home, I came to the church and asked our Impact Church worship leaders to join me in writing a new worship song. My speech was still slurry. My brain was still blurry. And the right side of my body was still totally numb. But I sat down at the piano, I started playing, and we began writing a song.

My right hand was so heavy that I couldn't help but hit every bad note, but we kept writing. I couldn't see the keys because I was crying the entire time, but we kept writing. Our voices were shaking, but we kept writing. And we all bawled, but we kept writing.

We still didn't know what was going to happen. Things were uncertain, the future was unclear, and we didn't know if I would ever get better, or if things would stay this way for the rest of my life. But we worshipped despite our worry, despite our fear, and despite the circumstances. And it was exactly what I needed.

It was such a powerful moment, worshipping God together. It was also really healing. And when we were finished, what we had was more than a song, it was the anthem of my life.

I want to close this chapter by sharing the lyrics of that song with you today:

"But I'm Still Standing" by Impact Worship

He can do anything
He can do everything
He's able to do it all

God of exceedingly
God of abundantly
Above what we ask or think

My healing is another chance
My healing is another chance
To say

Hallelujah
Hallelujah
Hallelujah
To God be glory

Your grace is all I need
Sufficient perfect peace
My eyes have yet not seen

Best days ahead of me
The devil thought he had me
Jesus is all need

My healing is another chance
My healing is another chance
To say
Hallelujah
Hallelujah
Hallelujah
To God be glory

Just be still
Stay with God
And watch him move
Just be still
Stay with God
Watch him move

But I'm still standing
But I'm still standing
But I'm still standing
He's got me through

Key Scriptures:

"Stay alert! Watch out for your great enemy, the devil. He prowls around like a roaring lion, looking for someone to devour." 1 Peter 5:8 (NLT)

"For our struggle is not against flesh and blood, but against the rulers, against the authorities, against the powers of this dark world and against the spiritual forces of evil in the heavenly realms." Ephesians 6:12 (NIV)

"No weapon formed against you shall prosper..." Isaiah 54:17 (NKJV)

"What then shall we say to these things? If God is for us, who can be against us?" Romans 8:31 (ESV)

Let's Pray:

Father, we know that our struggle is not against flesh and blood, and we ask that You would help us to keep our focus on the right enemy and the right fight. Today, I lift up those who are fighting battles, those who are beat up, beat down, and under attack. God, I pray that You would be their strength and their shield. That You would make them strong and courageous. And that You would help them to stand firmly and securely on Your Word, knowing that no weapon formed against them will prosper, and that He who is in them is greater than he who is in the world. We know that You have never lost a battle, and you're not losing this one, either. We love You, Jesus. We pray this in Your mighty name, amen.

Chapter 10

FROM MISERY TO MINISTRY

"You intended to harm me, but God intended
it all for good. He brought me to this position so I could
save the lives of many people."
– Genesis 50:20 (NLT)

I decided early on that I wasn't going to let the devil gain even an inch of territory as a result of my stroke. Instead, I was going to fight back. So, I continued pushing forward with my therapy, and also took the opportunity to do anything and everything else that doctors would allow.

One of those things was to go right back to doing Phoenix Suns chapel. I wasn't able to drive yet, and we still had to monitor my health very closely, but doctors agreed that it would be good for me to have some sort of normalcy and to do something familiar that resembled my old routine.

My son, Josiah, drove me down to the arena for every home game, and he sat next to me and supported me through every single chapel. My speech was still slurred. My words were still jumbled. And I would often lose my train of thought in the middle of a sentence and have to ask Josiah to jump in and explain what I was trying to say.

But because it was the Phoenix Suns family, it was the perfect place for me to keep doing what I do. They let me struggle. They let me relearn. They let me rehabilitate. And from the moment that I stepped foot back into that arena, they were all extremely supportive and showed me so much love.

One moment that was so special to me happened on my first day back. I was walking through the family room area of the arena when I noticed Devin Booker's father, Melvin Booker, across the room. He was probably 20 yards away, and there were a ton of people between us, but as soon as he saw me, he beelined it over to me, threw his arms out, and gave me the biggest hug. He said

"Pastor, I'm so glad you're alive. We need you. This world needs you. Do not go anywhere... and keep fighting."

His encouragement in that moment was so meaningful to me. All I could do was stand there in the middle of the arena and cry. It was just so good for me to be there, and I really believe that it was instrumental to my healing.

First night back at Suns chapel

Something else that I started working on almost immediately was writing a sermon. It was difficult because my hand was numb, and I really couldn't type. I remember sending a text to my wife because I was so frustrated with the process. But she encouraged me to keep going, so I kept working at it.

And just one month after I was released from the hospital, not only did I finish that sermon, I actually preached it. It was a Christmas Eve message that I recorded on video, and I did it in just one take, which was shocking considering I couldn't even speak not long before that.

My second message back was three weeks later, on January 15, 2023. This time, I preached live and in person, with my blood pressure monitor and emergency medication ready backstage.

Over the course of the next several months, I continued preaching every few weeks. I still couldn't type. It took me ten times longer than normal to put my messages together. I was totally numb on the entire right side of my body, and I could not feel my tongue or cheek. But the devil had targeted my calling, my very reason for existing, and this was a personal fight.

So, I came out swinging in Jesus' name. I decided to take everything that the enemy threw at me, all the hell he put me through, and flip it, turn it, and use it against him. And I decided to make my misery a ministry.

My text to Natalie as I tried to write my first sermon - so frustrated

When I think of turning misery into ministry, I think about the story of Joseph in the Bible. Remember earlier when we were talking about how bad things happen, even to good people? Well, that's Joseph.

Basically, Joseph was a really good guy that a lot of bad things happened to. He had 11 brothers, but he was clearly the favorite child and the dad made it super obvious. This caused a lot of issues for Joseph within the family, so while he may have been treated great by his dad, he had a very strained relationship with his siblings.

One day, Joseph's dad presented him with a one-of-a-kind, colorful coat. It was a totally extravagant gift in those days. And when Joseph's brothers saw it, they were filled with jealousy.

To make matters worse, Joseph started having crazy dreams that his brothers bowed down to him and made him their leader… and he actually told them about it. This put the brothers over the edge. They were so mad, so jealous, so full of spite toward Joseph, that they made a plan to kill him.

At the last minute, one of the brothers, Judah, had second thoughts. He convinced the others that it would be better for them to sell Joseph into slavery rather than commit murder, and they all agreed. So, as a caravan passed by, they sold Joseph to some merchants, and he ended up in Egypt working as a slave in a royal house.

The Bible says that the Lord was with Joseph, and he was successful in everything he did. In fact, he did such a good job that his master, Potiphar, eventually put him in charge of his entire household and everything he owned.

Things were going as well as could be expected in the situation, until Potiphar's wife started noticing Joseph. She attempted to seduce him, but when he rejected her, she lied, falsely accused him of coming after her, and had Joseph thrown into prison.

At this point, things were not looking good for Joseph. But this is where the story really starts to get interesting. Because while in prison, Joseph started interpreting dreams for people, and eventually, he interpreted a dream for Pharaoh, the most powerful person in all of Egypt.

Pharaoh was so pleased with Joseph that he promoted him to second in power...of the entire kingdom. What a rollercoaster. Joseph went from being a beloved son, to a betrayed brother, to a slave in a foreign land, to a prisoner, to the man in charge of it all.

And that's not even the best part of the story. Because after Joseph took his new position, a terrible famine came upon the land, and God used Joseph to save not one, but two nations from destruction and starvation. Millions of people had their lives spared, all thanks to Joseph.

Eventually, Joseph's brothers traveled to Egypt in search of food and they all ended up face to face. When the brothers finally realized who he was, they threw themselves at his feet hoping he would show them mercy. And do you know what Joseph did? He forgave them, he showed them mercy, and then he made this powerful statement:

"You intended to harm me, but God intended it all for good. He brought me to this position so I could save the lives of many people." (Genesis 50:20, NLT)

Wow. What incredible perspective. Joseph was looking at things through an eternal mindset. He knew that his trial wasn't just about him. He knew that God had a bigger plan and a bigger purpose in mind, and that the same weapon the devil tried to use against him was the very same weapon that God used to accomplish so much good.

Did you know that the same is true of your life and my life too? It's true for our trials and our fires. It's true for our valleys and our storms. It's true for our hard times and our tough situations. God can take the very thing that was meant to destroy us, and turn it for something good.

———

I've learned that one of the many ways that God uses our pain is by giving us a ministry to help others. I think sometimes people assume that ministry is a church word. That it's reserved for the pastor, rabbi, pope or priest. But the word minister really just means "to serve," and every single one of us is called to be in ministry.

When we use our pain in ministry, it simply means that we help others who are struggling with the same things that we've struggled with. We use our hurts to help heal them. We use our brokenness to help put them back together. We use our discouragements to help encourage them. We use our past to help rewrite their future. And we use what has bound us to help set them free.

I think 2 Corinthians 1:3-4 (NLT) sums this up really well. It says: "All praise to God, the Father of our Lord Jesus Christ. God is our merciful Father and the source of all comfort. He comforts us in all our troubles so that we can comfort others. When they are troubled, we will be able to give them the same comfort God has given us."

I love this same passage in the Message translation. It says "... He comes alongside us when we go through hard times, and before you know it, he brings us alongside someone else who is going through hard times so that we can be there for that person just as God was there for us."

In other words, there is just no one better to help somebody through something, than somebody who's already been through something. It's really that simple.

Think about it. Who is better equipped to help someone with drug addiction, than somebody who has conquered drug addiction. Who can better relate to an alcoholic, than someone who has experienced victory over alcoholism. Who can better walk alongside somebody diagnosed with cancer, than somebody else who's been diagnosed with cancer. And who can better understand someone who's lost a loved one, than somebody who's lost a loved one.

It is incredibly comforting and encouraging to others when you say this is where I've struggled, this is how I made it through, and if you need help, I'm going to walk with you because I know that you can have victory too.

I think we really underestimate just how important this is, and many of us don't do it. For some reason, we don't want anyone to know about our problems. We would rather leave the past buried in the past. But God wants us to do the exact opposite.

Revelation 12:11 (NIV) says "They triumphed over him by the blood of the Lamb and by the word of their testimony..." What does that mean? It means that there's no power in a testimony that's hidden. The power is in sharing the story about what God has done in your life.

In fact, there's not a more powerful tool that you have than your story. Nobody can deny it. You lived it, walked it out, and survived it. God got you through it, you have the scars to prove it, and no one can tell you otherwise.

By the way, it's amazing what happens when you're humble and honest about the struggles you've had. People are endeared to you. They see the realness in you. They're drawn to you. And as a result, your struggles become one of the most powerful ministries you could ever have.

———

I know that right now, some of you are probably thinking that you don't have much of a story. Or maybe you feel like your story isn't as impactful as someone else's. Here's the thing. There's not one of us who hasn't been through something in life. And if you are alive and reading this right now, then God has gotten you through and you have a story to tell.

Paul said: "The human body has many parts, but the many parts make up one whole body. So it is with the body of Christ... If the whole body were an eye, how would you hear? Or if your whole body were an ear, how would you smell anything? But our bodies have many parts, and God has put each part just where he wants it...In fact, some parts of the body that seem weakest and least important are actually the most necessary." (1 Corinthians 12:12, 17-18, 22, NLT)

In other words, your story is needed. You know things that not everyone knows. You have lived through things that not everyone has lived through. You have an upbringing, skill set, connections, and resources that others don't have. And what you have been through and experienced is exactly what someone else needs.

———

I can't tell you how many people I have been able to minister to because I had a hemorrhagic stroke. I've been sharing my story with anybody and everybody who will listen. And the more that I've shared, the more opportunities God has given me to share.

I've shared my story with everyone from complete strangers to close friends, and everywhere from hospital waiting rooms to the church stage to the Phoenix Suns chapel. And check this out. God is so good that my story was featured on every single local Arizona news station, and even ended up on the front page of the Arizona Republic sports section.

Every chance I get to speak, I'm making sure that everyone hears what God has done. I want them to know that there is hope when they feel helpless. There is healing when they are hurting. And there is a way when there seems to be no way.

I want them to know that God is our deliverer and redeemer. He is our healer and our restorer. He is our stability in the storm. He is our way maker and miracle worker. And nothing is impossible with Him!

I'm giving all glory to God. And I don't ever plan to stop. I will continue to share my story because I want everyone to know, and I'll shout it out for all to hear – what He's done for me, He can do for you!

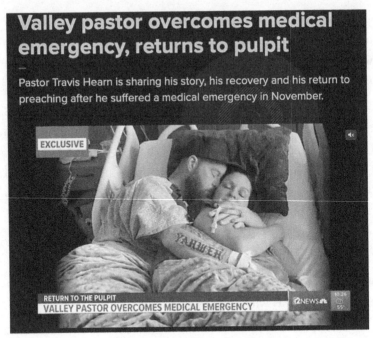

January 8, 2023 Channel 12 News

January 13, 2023 Arizona's Family

February 3, 2023 AZ Central

If you are going through a trial today, I want you to know that, too. What He's done for me, He can do for you. This trial is not your final destination. Your current pain has a purpose. And your past trials were not a waste.

God is preparing you. He is equipping you. He's bigger than your trial and this thing that is hurting you. He can turn your pain into a new purpose. Your mess into a message of hope. Your test into a testimony. And your misery into a ministry!

Arizona Republic | FRIDAY, FEBRUARY 3, 2023 | 1B

USA TODAY SPORTS

SPORTS

Inside
The Diamondbacks have sold advertising space on their jerseys, 5B

Impact Church senior pastor Travis Hearn serves as the team chaplain to the Suns. Hearn suffered a serious stroke late last year and has recovered enough to return to preaching and ministering. ALEX GOULD/THE REPUBLIC

Suns chaplain renews purpose after stroke

Dana Scott
Arizona Republic
USA TODAY NETWORK

Pro athletes and their head coaches endure a lot of stress. They also can have a spiritual connection to their game and life away from it.

For the Suns, team chaplain Travis Hearn helps players and coaches confront with the anxieties that can surface before and after their games.

"I feel like we all are created on purpose and for a purpose. I think the people who are the happiest on Earth and the most fulfilled in earth in life, they know what they're built to do," Hearn told The Republic.

Hearn himself found renewed purpose late last year, after suffering a serious stroke that left him unable to speak. But he recovered enough to return to his ministry.

"When you're in a sweet spot of doing what you're built to do, that's where you find so much joy and so much life. For me, ministry is about helping people. It's about helping the hurting, and hurting all around us."

The 48-year-old Hearn, or "PT" for Pastor Travis as his closest associates and the Suns call him, has been the team's minister since 2002. He runs their game-day chapel services one hour before every home game, where players or coaches can pray with him before they enter the court. He also holds Bible studies.

"It provides a moment of clarity and perspective. You play this game, and for us it's a means to feed our families and fulfill my purpose," Suns general manager James Jones told The Republic.

"So when you walk into the building, typically from the moment you come down to rim, you're focused on the game and that's the biggest thing in your life. But PT just provides us a moment of clarity where we can have perspective in realize there are things way bigger than us, that life is bigger than the game of basketball," Jones said. "Doing life and navigating life with people who understand that, believe there are higher purposes for us as beings. It's cool because it just gives you that balance that you need to be stable and be successful in this sport."

Visiting team members are welcome to attend the pregame chapel services Hearns holds as well.

"The one cool thing about the NBA is that every team opens that door up for all the players time to pray whether you're Christian or not," Suns coach Monty Williams told The Republic.

Williams said he met Hearn 20 years ago before he retired as an NBA player. Their spiritual bond grew stronger when Williams was hired as the Suns head coach in May 2019.

Williams, a devout Christian, has been attending pregame chapels

See **CHAPLAIN, Page 4B**

SUPER BOWL 57

Tillman set to be honored at game

Jeremy Cluff
Arizona Republic
USA TODAY NETWORK

Pat Tillman will be honored before Super Bowl 57 in Arizona on Feb. 12, the NFL has announced.

The league has selected four Pat Tillman Foundation Tillman Scholars that "represent the enduring legacy of service that Pat Tillman left behind" to serve as honorary coin toss captains before the game between the Kansas City Chiefs and Philadelphia Eagles at State Farm Stadium.

The four honorary captains are military spouse and Ed.D. candidate Fabersha Flynt, U.S. Army veteran and filmmaker Robert Ham, U.S. Army

See **TILLMAN, Page 5B**

HIGH SCHOOL BASKETBALL

Chandler AZ Compass Prep senior Mookie Cook portrayed a young LeBron James in an upcoming movie. ROB SCHUMACHER/THE REPUBLIC

Cook embraced movie role as LeBron

February 3, 2023 Arizona Republic sports page cover

131

Key Scriptures:

"You intended to harm me, but God intended it all for good. He brought me to this position so I could save the lives of many people." Genesis 50:20 (NLT)

"All praise to God, the Father of our Lord Jesus Christ. God is our merciful Father and the source of all comfort. He comforts us in all our troubles so that we can comfort others. When they are troubled, we will be able to give them the same comfort God has given us." 2 Corinthians 1:3-4 (NLT)

"They triumphed over him by the blood of the Lamb and by the word of their testimony..." Revelation 12:11 (NIV)

Let's Pray:

Father, we're so grateful that our trials and our traumas are never the end of the story, that Your ways are higher than our ways, and that You always have a bigger plan, and a bigger purpose, for our pain. Today, I pray for those who have been holding back and have been hesitant to share their stories. I ask that You would fill them with confidence and courage, knowing that their experiences and what they have been through could be exactly what someone else needs. Thank You for turning our pain into a new purpose, our mess into a message of hope, our test into a testimony, and our misery into a ministry to help others! We love You, Jesus. We pray this in Your mighty name, amen.

Chapter 11

A NEW MISSION FIELD

"But how can people call for help if they don't know who to trust? And how can they know who to trust if they haven't heard of the One who can be trusted? And how can they hear if nobody tells them? And how is anyone going to tell them, unless someone is sent to do it?"
– Romans 10:14 (MSG)

Do you want to know something amazing that's happened as a result of this stroke? God has opened doors that I would have never been able to walk through, put me in places that I would have never been able to go to, and placed me in front of people that I would have never been able to meet, had I not gone through it.

And because of that, I've been able to share Jesus and His love in places and ways that I never have before. It's almost like a whole new world has been opened to me. A world that I never would have visited or even known existed.

And that's one thing that I've learned about trials. Often, what looks like adversity is really just an opportunity in disguise. And what looks like a setback is really just a setup for God to use us in ways we never could have imagined.

––––––––––

There is no one in the Bible who knows more about this than Paul. Paul, also known as Saul, started out persecuting Christians and wanted to have them all killed. But eventually, Paul became a Christian himself, and he started lighting the world on fire for Jesus.

Paul began traveling around, preaching and planting churches, and many people were getting saved and healed. This upset the leaders at the time and they wanted to stop the message from spreading, so they threw Paul into prison.

Now check out how Paul responded. He decided that nothing was going to stop him, and if he couldn't speak it, he would write it. So, Paul began writing letters from prison. And do you know what happened to those letters? They became so influential to the Christian faith that 2,000 years later we're still reading them today.

If you've read any of the New Testament, you've most likely read some of the writings of Paul. In fact, two-thirds of its 27 books came from him. But, if Paul hadn't been thrown into prison, and if he hadn't faced the things that he did, he wouldn't have written those letters. And if he hadn't written those letters, we would not have them as part of God's Word as we know it today.

─────

Prison wasn't the only hardship Paul dealt with. In fact, he faced multiple kinds of trials. In 2 Corinthians 11, we read that Paul was whipped, beaten, stoned, and left for dead. He experienced starvation, thirst, and hunger. There were times he didn't have enough clothes to put on his back to keep him warm. He experienced not one, not two, but three separate shipwrecks. And he was also beaten with 39 lashes five different times.

Why are 39 lashes significant? Because 40 was known to kill a man. Back in Bible times, when you received lashes as a punishment, they used a special whip that had pieces of bone and rock tied to it. It would literally take the skin off your back. 39 lashes brought you one lash from death. And 40 was illegal.

I think we can all agree that Paul went through some of the worst trials we could imagine. Just one of them would be enough to take most of us out. That's why I find it so amazing that during this time, Paul wrote some of the very same verses that encourage and comfort us in our trials today.

It's Paul who wrote, "I can do all things through Christ who strengthens me." (Philippians 4:13, NKJV)

"No, in all these things we are more than conquerors through him who loved us." (Romans 8:37, NIV)

"That's why I take pleasure in my weaknesses, and in the insults, hardships, persecutions, and troubles that I suffer for Christ. For when I am weak, then I am strong." (2 Corinthians 12:10, NLT)

"What, then, shall we say in response to these things? If God is for us, who can be against us?" (Romans 8:31, NIV)

"For we walk by faith, not by sight." (2 Corinthians 5:7, NKJV)

"I have fought the good fight, I have finished the race, I have kept the faith." (2 Timothy 4:7, NIV)

"For to me, to live is Christ and to die is gain." (Philippians 1:21, NIV)

―――――――

One of my favorite stories about Paul is in Acts chapter 16. In it, we read that after Paul and Silas delivered a demon-possessed woman, they were stripped, severely beaten, and thrown into prison. And not just the regular prison. They were thrown into the innermost dungeon, where the worst of the worst criminals were sent.

These guys found themselves in a really bad situation. But do you know how they responded? Instead of despairing over their circumstances, the Bible says that Paul and Silas began to pray and sing praises to God. And in Acts 16:25 (NLT) we read that "the other prisoners were listening."

Suddenly, there was a violent earthquake that shook the prison so hard, all the prison doors flew open, and the prisoners' chains came loose. The jailer woke up, came running in, and when he realized what had happened, he drew his sword and was about to kill himself because he thought the prisoners had escaped.

But check this out. "... Paul shouted, 'Don't harm yourself! We are all here!' The jailer called for lights, rushed in and fell trembling before Paul and Silas. He then brought them out and asked, 'Sirs, what must I do to be saved?'" (Acts 16:28-30, NIV) And he and his entire family were saved and baptized that very night.

There are so many things that I love about this story.

I love that Acts 16:25 points out that the other prisoners were listening. Because when you're going through hell, there will always be others around you watching. And some of them might be going through hell, too.

I also love that they decided to praise God regardless of their circumstances. Because that can be hard for some of us to do. When we're in a dark place, it can be so tempting to gripe and complain. And yet, here they were, in the middle of their trial, taking an opportunity to praise.

And then, I love that all the doors flew open and everyone's chains came loose. Sometimes, we get so entrenched and trapped in our own prison and our own situation that we can't think of anything else but ourselves. But our trials are never just about us.

In Philippians 1:12-14 (NLT), Paul said: "And I want you to know, my dear brothers and sisters, that everything that has happened to me here has helped to spread the Good News. For everyone here, including the whole palace guard, knows that I am in chains because of Christ. And because of my imprisonment, most of the believers here have gained confidence and boldly speak God's message without fear."

He's saying, "I got locked up to set people free. Because I'm in prison, the gospel of Jesus Christ has spread. Because I'm in prison, other believers are gaining confidence!" And listen. Because of our trials, great things are going to happen, too!

I have absolutely seen that. So many incredible things have happened BECAUSE of my stroke. And one of those things is that I have been able to share Jesus in places and in ways that I never have before.

I have been blown away at how God has used this stroke to give me opportunity after opportunity to share Jesus and His love with people I would have never even met.

I've spent time in hospitals, doctor's offices, and therapy centers. I've met countless doctors, physical therapists, speech therapists, specialists, and nurses. I've met many people who were receiving treatment and therapy just like I was. And because of my trial, because of my stroke, I was right there in the middle of it all, and I had the chance to share.

Check this out. My speech therapist and doctor even asked if I wanted to preach parts of my sermons to them to practice getting my speech back on track. Ummm, yes! How cool is that!?

And do you know what I find really exciting? If you are holding this book in your hands today, God has given me the opportunity to share Jesus with you. We may never meet each other in person. You may never visit Impact Church, or watch a message online, and you may never plan to. But because of my trial, God has given me this opportunity to share my story, and share His love, with you.

═══════

You may be thinking to yourself, "Well Pastor Trav, of course you're out sharing Jesus, you're a pastor, that's what you do." But just because I'm a pastor doesn't mean I'm the only one who's supposed to be doing this. You are too. Building the Kingdom of God isn't only up to the preachers of the world, it's up to the people of the world.

If you know Jesus as your Lord and Savior, you're not meant to keep it to yourself. You're meant to share it. In fact, some of the final words of Jesus, after He died and rose again on the third day, were: "Go into all the world and preach the gospel to all creation." (Mark 16:15, NIV)

This wasn't a command directed only to certain people. This was a command for all of us. God wants us to be a voice, heart, hands, and feet for Him.

In Romans 10:14 (MSG), Paul says: "But how can people call for help if they don't know who to trust? And how can they know who to trust if they haven't heard of the One who can be trusted? And how can they hear if nobody tells them? And how is anyone going to tell them, unless someone is sent to do it?"

I love that it says, "how is anyone going to tell them, unless someone is sent to do it." I think that's such a powerful way that we can look at our trials.

Think about it: how differently would we experience our trials if we viewed them as somewhere that we've been sent? If we saw every new situation that we stepped into as a potential mission field? If we treated the people we met along the way as if God Himself placed them there on purpose, for a purpose?

Paul goes on to say in Romans 10:15b (NLT) "…How beautiful are the feet of messengers who bring good news!" And guess what. If you know Jesus…that's you. You bring good news!

When you walk into trials, difficulties, hard times, and dark places, you walk in carrying good news. In fact, you carry the greatest news that you could ever share. And there will always be people around you who desperately need to hear it.

People who need to hear that Jesus is the answer to the sick and the broken. That He's the answer to the lonely and the depressed. That He's the answer to the drug addict and the alcoholic. That He's the answer to the hopeless and the helpless. And that He is the answer to set people free.

The sobering truth is that we are the only Jesus that some people will ever see. We are the only Jesus that some people will ever hear. And we could change someone's eternal destination just by sharing. That's what it's all about!

If you've never surrendered your life to Jesus Christ, I'd like to give you an opportunity to do that today. It's the best decision you could ever make, and I've never met anyone who regretted it.

Romans 10:9 (ESV) says that "if you confess with your mouth that Jesus is Lord and believe in your heart that God raised him from the dead, you will be saved." So, let's do that together right now. Pray:

Dear Jesus, today, I give You my life. I want to live for You because You died for me. Thank you for dying on the cross to pay the price for my sins. Thank You for forgiveness, grace, mercy, and unconditional love. Today, I acknowledge You as my personal Lord and Savior. Please help me, teach me, and encourage me as I seek to know and grow closer to You. I love You, Jesus. I pray this in Your name, Amen.

If you just prayed that prayer, I'm so proud of you and I'm so happy to say: Congratulations and welcome to the family of God!

Key Scriptures:

"But how can people call for help if they don't know who to trust? And how can they know who to trust if they haven't heard of the One who can be trusted? And how can they hear if nobody tells them? And how is anyone going to tell them, unless someone is sent to do it?" Romans 10:14 (MSG)

"'He said to them, 'Go into all the world and preach the gospel to all creation.'" Mark 16:15 (NIV)

"And I want you to know, my dear brothers and sisters, that everything that has happened to me here has helped to spread the Good News. For everyone here, including the whole palace guard, knows that I am in chains because of Christ. And because of my imprisonment, most of the believers here have gained confidence and boldly speak God's message without fear." Philippians 1:12-14 (NLT)

"...How beautiful are the feet of messengers who bring good news!" Romans 10:15b (NLT)

Let's Pray:

Father, we know that You are the answer to all of the world's problems, and that true peace, true joy, true comfort, true healing, true purpose, and true meaning can only be found in You. Help us to be fearless in sharing these truths with others, and to see each new person, new place, and new situation that we encounter as an opportunity to be a heart, hands, feet, and voice for You. God, Your Word says, "how beautiful are the feet of messengers who bring good news" and we ask that You would help us to be those messengers today. We love you, Jesus. We pray this in Your mighty name, amen.

Chapter 12

THE FIRE IS FOR YOU

"I have refined you, but not as silver is refined. Rather, I have refined you in the furnace of suffering."
– Isaiah 48:10 (NLT)

This whole experience has been full of open doors and new opportunities to reach the world around me. But God has also been using this stroke, and everything that I've been through as a result of this stroke, to make some big changes within me.

My mind has changed. My heart has changed. My outlook has changed. My perspective has changed. And I will absolutely never look at life the same way again.

It's been difficult. I've learned some painful lessons. But I now see that what felt hard and even unbearable at times, was actually really good for me. And so many of the things that I went through were all a part of God's process of refining me.

———

The Bible actually talks a lot about this. In fact, there are many instances where God's Word compares life's trials to refineries.

Isaiah 48:10 (NLT) says "I have refined you, but not as silver is refined. Rather, I have refined you in the furnace of suffering."

1 Peter 1:7 (NLT) tells us "These trials will show that your faith is genuine. It is being tested as fire tests and purifies gold – though your faith is far more precious than mere gold..."

And Psalm 66:10 (NIV) says "For you, God, tested us; you refined us like silver."

———

The process used to refine precious metal in Bible times was actually really interesting. First, they would take big rocks that held promise of having silver inside, and they would break the rocks into pieces. Then, they would place the pieces in a melting pot and expose the pot to fire. As the fire grew hotter and hotter, the impurities and cheap metals in the rocks melted and rose to the top, where the refiner would scrape them off, revealing the precious metal underneath.

This process continued several times over until all of the impurities were clear. There were some impurities, however, that only came out at a certain temperature. So, as a final step, they would heat the fire seven times hotter, and repeat. The process was finally complete when the refiner could see their own reflection, their own image, in the precious metal.

Many of us go through seasons and situations in life that feel a lot like this process. Our pains, problems, hurts, and failures break us down. We're under fire in our relationships, our emotions, our health or our finances. We're feeling the heat, feeling the pressure, and we just don't think we can take any more.

We may wonder why God is allowing us to go through this, but the Bible tells us that these are the moments, and this is the process, that God uses to refine us.

He allows us to be broken so that he can dig all of the gold and silver out of us. He turns up the heat a little hotter because He knows it will burn the impurities out of us. And ultimately, His goal is to see His reflection in us.

———

As humans, this concept can be really difficult for us. We don't like to feel any type of pain. In fact, most of us do anything and everything we can to avoid it. But we all need refining, and even the most well-known heroes of the Bible went through it.

In fact, David talked about this in Psalm 119:67 (NIV) when he said "Before I was afflicted I went astray, but now I obey your word." A few verses later, in Psalm 119:71-72 (NLT) he went on to say "My suffering was good for me, for it taught me to pay attention to your decrees. Your instructions are more valuable to me than millions in gold and silver."

I love that he said, "My suffering was good for me." It reminds me of when I was younger, and an athlete playing sports. My coach would always say "no pain, no gain." And that is true in sports. But I think that's also pretty true when it comes to a lot of things in life. Without some pain, without some hurts, without some problems, there would be no gains.

I have definitely experienced this throughout the recovery process of my stroke. Especially when it comes to physical therapy and the work it took to restore strength and ability to my body. But I've also experienced this many times throughout my life.

I know that some of the most valuable lessons that I've ever learned in life came on the other side of suffering and misery. And some of the most worthwhile things that I've built came after a labor of blood, sweat, tears, heartache, and pain.

The truth is, if we want God's promises and we want God's product, we are going to have to go through God's process. In fact, nowhere in life will you see a finished product that has not undergone some type of process. And that process was probably not pain free.

A pearl is the perfect example of this. Have you ever thought about how a pearl is made?

It all begins when an irritant, like a piece of sand or a parasite, makes its way inside of an oyster. This bothers the oyster so much, that the oyster responds by releasing a fluid that coats the irritant to make it less painful. This coating process happens over and over again, layer after layer, until eventually, a pearl is created.

The beautiful, unique, and highly sought after pearl is really the end result of a process of constant irritation, frustration, and agitation. If there was never any irritant, there would be no pearl. No hard times, no pearl. No friction, no pearl. No painful process, no pearl.

And that's really the way it goes in your life and my life, too. We go through fires, trials, hardships, and difficulties. We go through things that irritate us, pain us, crush us, and make us miserable. But without that pain, and without that process, we would never become everything that God made us to be.

When we think of becoming everything we're meant to be, we tend to think in terms of worldly things. We think about family and career. We think about achievements and success. We think about lifestyle and money. We think about what we need to do, and what we need to accomplish, in order to be comfortable.

But God is much more interested in our character than our comfort. And what He wants for our lives is to see His character in us. Ezekiel 36:26 (NIV) says "I will give you a new heart and put a new spirit in you; I will remove from you your heart of stone and give you a heart of flesh."

God wants to give us the same heart He has. He wants us to love like He loves, to give like He gives, to serve like He served, to surrender like He surrendered, and to sacrifice like He sacrificed. And He's always working on our behalf with that goal in mind.

Romans 8:28 (NIV) says "And we know that in all things God works for the good of those who love him, who have been called according to his purpose."

In all things. That means that in the good and the bad, the hard and the painful, and the highs, lows, and plateaus, God is at work. And He's not only working in our trials, our circumstances, and our situations. He's using our trials, our circumstances, and our situations to accomplish His great work in us.

———

Sometimes, the thing that we think is going to destroy us, is the very thing that God is using to teach us, develop us, redirect us, grow us, change us, and make us more like Him. Think about it like this:

The fire that we're facing, may be what God is using to purify our lives. The heat may feel unbearable. It may seem like it's more than we can take. But God knows exactly what we need. And He knows the exact temperature it will take to remove the pollutants that are toxic and dangerous for us.

The valley that we're walking through, may be what God is using to redirect our path. Things may look bleak. It may seem like we're totally lost and completely off course. But God sees the way when there seems to be no way. And sometimes, He leads us through a valley to get us on the path to victory.

The pain and pressure that we're under, may be what God is using to prepare us for our purpose. We may feel like we're getting the squeeze of our lives, it might seem like we're about to break.

But God knows what that pressure is about to produce. And just like a diamond cannot be made without it, there are some things in our lives that will only come to be as a result of extreme pressure.

The crushing that we're going through, may be what God is using to break down our walls and soften our hearts. It may seem like there's no way any good could come from our situation. But with God, there is never a pain in vain. And He wants to use this trial to make us more humble, gentle, and loving. More tenderhearted, merciful, and kind. More giving, serving, and thoughtful. And ultimately more like Him.

Now, I feel like I need to say this next part, even though it isn't easy to hear: sometimes living out God's best for your life, and God does have a best for your life, might mean living through some of life's hardest and worst.

Even Jesus experienced this. In Luke 22, we read that He was in the Garden of Gethsemane, facing death on the cross, when "He walked away, about a stone's throw, and knelt down and prayed, 'Father, if you are willing, please take this cup of suffering away from me. Yet I want your will to be done, not mine.' Then an angel from heaven appeared and strengthened him. He prayed more fervently, and he was in such agony of spirit that his sweat fell to the ground like great drops of blood." (Luke 22:41-44, NLT)

Think about Jesus for a minute. He suffered far more emotional and physical pain than any other human in the history of the world. He experienced betrayal, hatred, mockery, rejection, and humiliation. He was crucified and died a brutal death on the cross. Why?

So that you and I would receive eternal life. So that we would receive salvation.

There would be no resurrection if it wasn't for the cross. And the truth is, there are some blessings in our lives that will only come through brokenness. There are some purposes that will only come through pain. And there are some things that will only come together when it feels like our whole world is falling apart.

———

That's why James said, "Count it all joy, my brothers, when you meet trials of various kinds." (James 1:2, ESV) He's not saying count it all joy because of what's happening in our trials, he's saying count it all joy because of what's going to come out of them.

Paul talked about this when he said "We also have joy with our troubles, because we know that these troubles produce patience. And patience produces character, and character produces hope." (Romans 5:3-4, NCV)

I'll admit. I haven't met many people who were joyful when they were going through hell. But these verses are saying that as men and women of God, not only can we be, we're really supposed to be. We may not feel joyful for our situation, but we can still be joyful in it because we know that this is all a part of God's process of making us complete.

———

1 Peter 4:12 (NLT) says "Dear friends, don't be surprised at the fiery trials you are going through…"

The fact is, we're all going to go through fires in life. You may even be going through your own personal fire right now. Your emotions may be wrecked. Your state of mind may be destroyed. Your spirit may be crushed. I've been there ... often. In fact, there have been times in my life, including throughout this stroke, that have felt like one great big inferno.

But if I've been reminded of one thing it's this. With God, there are no wildfires, only controlled fires. And when life gets harder and hotter, He is getting ready to refine us, to pull the gold and silver from inside of us, and to burn the impurities away.

Philippians 1:6 (NLT) says "And I am certain that God, who began the good work within you, will continue his work until it is finally finished on the day when Christ Jesus returns."

So, remember. Sometimes the very thing that's discouraging you is what God is using to develop you. The fire is actually for you. And He's not done with you yet!

Key Scriptures:

"I have refined you, but not as silver is refined. Rather, I have refined you in the furnace of suffering." Isaiah 48:10 (NLT)

"And we know that in all things God works for the good of those who love him, who have been called according to his purpose." Romans 8:28 (NIV)

"And I am certain that God, who began the good work within you, will continue his work until it is finally finished on the day when Christ Jesus returns." Philippians 1:6 (NLT)

Let's Pray:

Father, we know that You love us so much that You're always working on us, and that You're not done with us yet. Today, I pray for those who are in the fires of life. Remind them that this fire is for them, not against them, and that You always have a higher intention and a higher purpose in mind. Give them a new outlook and a new perspective, knowing that You are using this fire to purify them, refine them, grow them, change them, and ultimately, make them more like You. We know that He who began a good work in us will be faithful to complete it, and we're so grateful for Your process of transformation in our lives. We love You, Jesus. We pray this in Your mighty name, amen.

Chapter 13

REVERSE-ABLE

"Now all glory to God, who is able, through his mighty power at work within us, to accomplish infinitely more than we might ask or think."

– Ephesians 3:20 (NLT)

When I think back on my time in the hospital, there are a lot of things that are still really hazy for me. But there are also some things that really stand out. And one of those things is the word "irreversible."

The doctors told my wife that she should get used to me being this way because the effects of my stroke were irreversible. My loss of speech…irreversible. My loss of memory…irreversible. My loss of feeling …irreversible. My loss of strength … irreversible.

But do you know what I've learned? You really need to be careful who you listen to. And I'm so thankful that I married a woman of God, and that Natalie knew not to listen to those doctors, because Natalie knew the truth.

The truth is: I am a walking, talking testimony of God reversing the irreversible.

The effects of my basal ganglia stroke are literally being reversed day by day, hour by hour, and moment by moment. My speech is coming back. My cognition is coming back. My feeling is coming back. My strength is coming back. And God has been reversing every single stroke effect that I've had.

Why? Because God is reverse-able. In fact, He kind of built His reputation on reversing things.

He healed the blind. He healed the deaf. He healed the lame. He raised dead things back to life. And we see over and over again that He is the God of reversals.

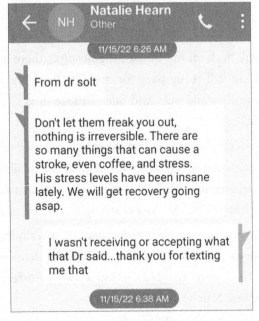

A message to Natalie from our friend and doctor, Dr. Solt

The Apostle Paul had an incredible experience with this. Now, if you don't know, Paul is my favorite person in the Bible next to Jesus Christ, and I've talked a lot about him throughout this book.

At first, Paul (also known as Saul) didn't believe in Jesus Christ. Even worse, he hated and persecuted anyone who did believe and tried to have them killed. He basically made it his life's mission to stop the gospel from spreading and going any further.

Until the day God flipped the script, pulled a reversal, and did a complete 180 in Paul's life.

You may be familiar with the story, but for those who aren't, let's do a quick recap:

In Acts chapter nine we read that one day Paul is out traveling, essentially hunting Christians, when:

"...A light from heaven suddenly shone down around him. He fell to the ground and heard a voice saying to him, 'Saul! Saul! Why are you persecuting me?' 'Who are you, lord?' Saul asked. And the voice replied, 'I am Jesus, the one you are persecuting! Now get up and go into the city, and you will be told what you must do.'" (Acts 9:3-6, NLT)

Paul gets up, opens his eyes, and it's then that he discovers that he's been struck completely blind. He can't see a thing. So, the men with him physically lead him to the city of Damascus where he sits and waits for three days.

Meanwhile, God gives a vision to a prophet, a believer named Ananias. He tells Ananias that he should go talk to Paul, lay hands on him, and pray so that he can see again.

At first, Ananias is totally freaked out. He knows exactly who Paul is and exactly what Paul is all about. In fact, his response in Acts 9:13 (MSG) is this: "Master, you can't be serious. Everybody's talking about this man and the terrible things he's been doing, his reign of terror against your people in Jerusalem!"

But, despite his fear, Ananias is obedient to God, goes out, finds Paul, and prays for him. And in Acts 9:18 (NLT) we read "Instantly something like scales fell from Saul's eyes, and he regained his sight. Then he got up and was baptized." Wow.

The Bible tells us that from this point on, Paul has a radically different outlook on life. He becomes a Christian. He starts spreading the gospel. He plants churches. And he writes two-thirds of the New Testament.

Talk about a complete reversal.

It's amazing that the same man who once tried to shut down the message of Christ, went on to shout out the message of Christ. The same man who once breathed murderous threats to the church, went on to grow and build the church. And the same man who was once a well-known persecutor, went on to become one of history's most well-known preachers.

I love this whole story because God didn't just pull one reversal, he pulled two. He not only reversed Paul's physical blindness, He reversed his spiritual blindness as well. And Paul received more than just his sight back, he also received God's divine vision and purpose for his life.

───────────

Even more than that, the Bible uses the word instantly. His physical issue was reversed, his spiritual issue was reversed, his entire life was changed, and it all happened instantly.

Man, I love this so much! Instantly. That's how fast God can turn your situation around.

He can reverse your health, your relationship, your financial situation, your emotions, your addiction, your depression, your anxiety, your heart, your mind, your life...and He can do it instantly.

It doesn't matter what your situation is. It doesn't matter how permanent it seems. God can reverse in one moment what you've been dealing with for a day, a decade, or even a lifetime.

Do you remember the story of Jesus healing the man who was blind?

In John chapter nine we read:

"As he went along, he saw a man blind from birth... he spit

on the ground, made some mud with the saliva, and put it on the man's eyes. 'Go,' he told him, 'wash in the Pool of Siloam' (this word means "Sent"). So the man went and washed, and came home seeing. His neighbors and those who had formerly seen him begging asked, 'Isn't this the same man who used to sit and beg?'" (John 9:1,6-8, NIV)

Notice that it says that the man was blind from birth? In other words, he had always known himself this way. Everyone else had always known him this way. His situation appeared to be permanent, lifelong, and irreversible.

But Jesus spit on the ground, made some mud, put it on the man's eyes, told him to go wash in the Pool of Siloam... and just like that, he was healed. Instantly, his blindness was reversed.

For some reason, when we read stories like this from the Bible, we think that they don't really apply to our lives today. But nothing could be further from the truth. God is still God, He still does reversals, and He is still reversing the irreversible even to this day!

———

Jeremiah 32:17 (NLT) says "O Sovereign LORD! You made the heavens and earth by your strong hand and powerful arm. Nothing is too hard for you!" I've seen this demonstrated time and time again in my own life. There really is nothing that God cannot do!

I am a part of a family bloodline where God has reversed generational curses. In my family, I've seen person after person come to Christ. I've seen alcoholics set free. I've seen drug addicts set free. And my mom was healed 100% of breast cancer.

In my church, I've seen God heal stage four cancer patients. I've seen Him raise marriages from the dead – even after a divorce happened. I've seen God bring the prodigal child home into His loving arms. And I've seen Him completely reverse the direction of people's lives.

And if you find yourself in what seems like an irreversible situation today, God can do the same for you. Your situation is one hundred percent reversible - because God is literally reverse-able.

You may look at your circumstances and think that there's no way things could possibly change, but I'm telling you that when God is involved, there's no way they could possibly stay the same.

———

Ephesians 3:20 (NLT) says "Now all glory to God, who is able, through his mighty power at work within us, to accomplish infinitely more than we might ask or think." Another translation of this same verse says that He is able to do "exceedingly abundantly above all that we ask or think."

I love that. It's one of my life verses, and it's also my favorite verse in the Bible. Why? Because I believe with everything in me that it's true.

I believe that God is able. That He is the God of the impossible. And that there is no situation, circumstance or problem that He cannot flip, change, reverse, overturn or undo.

I believe that God is powerful. That He is bigger than the biggest problems that we face. And that there's nothing that He cannot do.

And I believe that He is reverse-able. He did it for me. And if He did it for me, He can do it for you, too!

Working out at Glory Gains Gym just one year after being told that the effects of my stroke were "irreversible"

Key Scriptures:

"Instantly something like scales fell from Saul's eyes, and he regained his sight. Then he got up and was baptized." Acts 9:18 (NLT)

"O Sovereign LORD! You made the heavens and earth by your strong hand and powerful arm. Nothing is too hard for you!" Jeremiah 32:17 (NLT)

"Now all glory to God, who is able, through his mighty power at work within us, to accomplish infinitely more than we might ask or think." Ephesians 3:20 (NLT)

"Now to Him who is able to do exceedingly abundantly above all that we ask or think, according to the power that works in us." Ephesians 3:20 (NKJV)

Let's Pray:

Father, Your Word says that You are able to accomplish infinitely more than we might ask or think, and that all things are possible with You. I pray that as we read those words, our faith would rise, our expectations would increase, and we would be reminded of who You are and what You can do. Today, I lift up those whose situations seem to be impossible and irreversible. God, I ask that You would do miracles. That You would flip, change, reverse, fix, and undo things like only You can do. We know that Your supernatural power changes things, and we are believing for big changes today. We love You, Jesus. We pray this in Your mighty name, amen.

Chapter 14

THIS IS NOT THE END
OF THE STORY

"...This is what the LORD, the God of your ancestor
David, says: I have heard your prayer and seen your tears.
I will heal you..."
– 2 Kings 20:5 (NLT)

My favorite day of the week - Sunday at Impact Church

I still can't believe that I faced the trial of my life and nearly died after suffering a brain aneurysm and hemorrhagic stroke. But by the grace of God and His miraculous power, I am here today healthy, healed, and whole.

I have my speech, my cognition, my memory, and my movement. I'm writing again, preaching again, teaching again, songwriting again and singing again. I'm stronger and healthier than I've been in years. And the best part of all is that I'm just getting started.

I've experienced firsthand that just because something looks like it's done, doesn't actually mean that it's done. And just because it looks like it's over, doesn't actually mean that it's over. Because when God's not done, God's not done. And no situation, circumstance, trial, attack or spiritual force of evil could ever accomplish otherwise.

I love the story of Hezekiah in the Bible because I think it's such an amazing example of this.

In the book of 2 Kings, we read that Hezekiah was the son of a king named Ahaz. King Ahaz was a wicked king. He closed down the temple of God in Jerusalem, put pagan altars and idols up, and even sacrificed his own sons as worship to the pagan god Baal.

But when Ahaz finally died and Hezekiah became king, Hezekiah went in and totally cleaned house. He reopened the temple of God, he broke generational curses by undoing all of the wickedness of his father, and because of his heart for God and his strong leadership, revival came to Judah.

2 Kings 18:5-7 (NLT) says that "...There was no one like him among all the kings of Judah, either before or after his time. He remained faithful to the LORD in everything, and he carefully obeyed all the commands the LORD had given Moses. So the LORD was with him, and Hezekiah was successful in everything he did..."

But then, things in Hezekiah's life took a sudden turn. He became deathly ill, and not long after that, received terrible news from the prophet Isaiah who told him "...Set your affairs in order, for you are going to die. You will not recover from this illness." (2 Kings 20:1, NLT)

Wow. Can you imagine? One moment, Hezekiah was serving God faithfully and experiencing great success, and the very next moment, he was receiving some of the worst possible news of his life.

The Bible says that "When Hezekiah heard this, he turned his face to the wall and prayed to the Lord, 'Remember, O Lord, how I have always been faithful to you and have served you single-mindedly, always doing what pleases you.' Then he broke down and wept bitterly." (2 Kings 20:2-3, NLT)

There are two things that really stand out to me about Hezekiah's reaction:

First, it says that he turned his face to the wall. This is significant because Hezekiah would have been totally surrounded by people. The prophet himself, the doctors, the court officials, the court secretary, the valet, the staff, and many others would all have been in the room with him.

But Hezekiah wanted to be alone with God. And in turning to the wall, he was intentionally blocking out everyone, and everything, so that he could place all of his focus and attention on Him.

And second, the Bible tells us that he cried. In fact, it says that he wept bitterly. And I think that's important for us to note because many of us have the misconception that when it comes to our trials, we need to be tough, so we cannot or should not cry. But nowhere in the Bible does it say that.

Instead, Psalm 56:8 (NLT) tells us "You keep track of all my sorrows. You have collected all my tears in your bottle. You have recorded each one in your book." And in Psalm 20:1 (NLT) we read "In times of trouble, may the LORD answer your cry..." So, we know that our tears matter to God, and that He hears and answers our cries.

That's exactly what Hezekiah experienced. Because just two verses later, we read that as the prophet Isaiah was on his way out, before he had even made it past the courtyard, the Lord told him to turn around, go back, and give Hezekiah this message:

"...This is what the Lord, the God of your ancestor David, says: I have heard your prayer and seen your tears. I will heal you..." (2 Kings 20:5, NLT)

I think that's such a powerful phrase... "this is what the Lord says." Because the truth is, it really doesn't matter what the doctor says, the devil says, fear says, depression says, discouragement says, hopelessness says, anxiety says, your situation says or your trial says. What matters is what the Lord says. And although it looked like things were over for Hezekiah, the Lord said that this was not the end.

─────────

The prophet Isaiah recorded this same story about Hezekiah, and in Isaiah chapter 38, he tells us what happened next. Check this out – it's so powerful:

In Isaiah 38:9 (NIV) we read "A writing of Hezekiah king of Judah after his illness and recovery..." followed by a detailed account, written by Hezekiah, describing what had happened and praising God for all of the miracles that He had done. (Isaiah 38:9-20, NIV)

I love that! In recounting all that God had brought him through, Hezekiah created a reminder not only for himself, but for others, too. And it wasn't just a reminder of what God did, it was a reminder of what God would do.

———————

David definitely understood this concept. We all know the story of how he defeated Goliath, but do you remember what happened right before that?

Immediately after David volunteered to fight Goliath, King Saul had him brought in for a meeting and tried to talk him out of the whole thing. He told David: "Don't be ridiculous! There's no way you can fight this Philistine and possibly win! You're only a boy, and he's been a man of war since his youth." (1 Samuel 17:33, NLT)

I think most of us would have considered giving up right then. But not David. He wasn't discouraged or dissuaded at all. Instead, he was more confident than ever.

He said: "I have been taking care of my father's sheep and goats…When a lion or a bear comes to steal a lamb from the flock, I go after it with a club and rescue the lamb from its mouth. If the animal turns on me, I catch it by the jaw and club it to death. I have done this to both lions and bears, and I'll do it to this pagan Philistine, too, for he has defied the armies of the living God! The LORD who rescued me from the claws of the lion and the bear will rescue me from this Philistine!'" (1 Samuel 17:34-37, NLT)

What an incredible response.

David was saying "I may have never faced a giant exactly like this one before, but I have faced giants. And although this giant may be different, it really doesn't matter because it's still the same God. And the same God that brought me through, is the same God that will bring me through. And the same God that did it before, is the same God that will do it again."

David later wrote:

"But then I recall all you have done, O Lord; I remember your wonderful deeds of long ago." (Psalm 77:11, NLT)

And "Let all that I am praise the LORD; may I never forget the good things he does for me." (Psalm 103:2, NLT)

I've noticed that most of us tend to do the opposite of David. We find ourselves in bad situations. We pray for God to help us, heal us, deliver us, and save us. And when He does, we're excited about it, and we tell people about it for a little while, but then, we move on with our lives almost as if it never even happened in the first place. And the next time we face a trial? We go through the cycle all over again.

But it's so important that we remember the miracles of God in our lives, not only to maintain a heart of thankfulness for what He's done in the past, but to build our faith and fill us with confidence about what He's going to do in the future.

And that's really why I've been writing this book. I want it to serve as a record and a reminder, not only for myself, but also for you, of what God has done and what God can do.

Looking back, I am amazed at all that God has brought me through. He saved my life. He healed my body. He restored my mind. He brought me back to health. He did the impossible, reversed the irreversible, performed miracle after miracle, and He did it over and over again. And I never want to forget it.

And do you know what? I really believe that He's just getting started. I believe that my best days are in front of me, not behind me. That this is not the end of my story. And that God's not done.

About a year after my stroke, Impact Worship released a song called "Leave Some Room." It was really birthed out of everything that I went through, and in it we sing "This is not the end of the story, just another chapter for Your glory…"

I don't know what it is that you're up against today, but I do know this. I not only believe that for my life, I believe it for your life, too. God did not bring you this far just to leave you right here. And He wouldn't see you through just to say you're through.

Just like it wasn't the end of the story for Hezekiah. Just like it wasn't the end of the story for David. And just like it wasn't the end of the story for Jonah, Job, Joseph, Moses, Daniel, Shadrach, Meshach, Abednego, Paul, and so many others all throughout the Bible, this is not the end of the story for you.

Remember. When God's not done, God's not done. And all the forces of Hell cannot stop what God has ordained for your life!

My "bride or die," Natalie, and I

Key Scriptures:

"...This is what the Lord, the God of your ancestor David, says: I have heard your prayer and seen your tears. I will heal you..." 2 Kings 20:5 (NLT)

"In times of trouble, may the LORD answer your cry. May the name of the God of Jacob keep you safe from all harm." Psalm 20:1 (NLT)

"But then I recall all you have done, O Lord; I remember your wonderful deeds of long ago." Psalm 77:11 (NLT)

"Let all that I am praise the LORD; may I never forget the good things he does for me." Psalm 103:2 (NLT)

Let's Pray:

Father, we know that You always have a perfect plan and a perfect purpose for our lives, and that there's always more to the story with You. Remind us of that today, God. Encourage those who are discouraged. Lift up those who are down. And give those who feel like they're at the end of their story a renewed sense of hope and expectation for their future. Help them to see that their best days are in front of them, not behind them, and help them to trust You as the author of their lives. We love You, Jesus. We pray this in Your mighty name, amen.

Scan here to listen to "Leave Some Room" by Impact Worship

"Leave Some Room" by Impact Worship

In real time
I'm fighting the battle of my life
Trying to protect what is mine
I can't control it all

In this life
I won't always get it just right
Sufficient is grace You provide
You give so I can have

This is not the end of the story
Just another chapter for Your glory
More to be written
More worship from within

The peace I find within Your arms
Is something that I've never felt
The joy I find within Your life
Is something that I've never felt
You're not done
There's more to come
All the way to completion
You're not done

Now it's time
To trust the author of my life
In total surrender lift Him high
The name of Jesus Christ

This is not the end of the story
Just another chapter for Your glory
More to be written
More worship from within

The peace I find within Your arms
Is something that I've never felt
The joy I find within Your life
Is something that I've never felt
You're not done
There's more to come
All the way to completion
You're not done

This is what the Lord said
Write down everything that I've done
But leave some room
Cause I know He's not done

This Is Not the End of the Story

Take a look at all that I've done
But leave some room
Cause I know He's not done

Write down everything that I've done
But leave some room
Cause I know He's not done
Take a look at all that I've done
But leave some room
Cause I know He's not done

Leave some room
Cause I know He's not done
Leave some room
Cause I know He's not done

This is not the end of the story
Just another chapter for Your glory
More to be written
More worship from within

The peace I find within Your arms
Is something that I've never felt
The joy I find within Your life
Is something that I've never felt
You're not done
There's more to come
All the way to completion
You're not done

This is what the Lord said
Write down everything that I've done
But leave some room

Cause I know He's not done
Take a look at
All that I've done
But leave some room
Cause I know He's not done
Write down everything that I've done
But leave some room
Cause I know He's not done
Take a look at all that I've done
But leave some room
Cause I know He's not done

This is what the Lord said
This is what the Lord said
This is what the Lord said
Write down everything that I've done

Leave some room
Cause I know He's not done
Leave some room
Cause I know He's not done

EPILOGUE

To learn more about Travis Hearn, Impact Church, or Impact Worship, and to access your free gifts, scan here.

ABOUT TRAVIS HEARN

Travis Hearn is the Senior Pastor of Impact Church in Scottsdale, Arizona. He has served as the Phoenix Suns Team Chaplain since 2002, and previously served as chapel leader for the National Football League, Major League Baseball, and Minor League Baseball for over a decade.

Travis and his wife, Natalie, live in Arizona and have been married since 1998. Together, they have three children – Kylie, Josiah, and Jazzlyn.

In November of 2022, Travis suffered a life-threatening brain aneurysm and hemorrhagic stroke, followed by a miraculous recovery and healing. His story has been featured on various media and news outlets nationwide.

Made in the USA
Monee, IL
05 December 2024

72386212R00108